INSIGHT ⊙ GUIDES

EXPLORE

NEW ZEALAND

⦿ Walking Eye App

Your guide now includes a free eBook to your chosen destination, for the same great price as before. Simply download the Walking Eye App from the App Store or Google Play to access your free eBook.

HOW THE WALKING EYE APP WORKS

Through the Walking Eye App, you can purchase a range of eBooks and destination content. However, when you buy this book, you can download the corresponding eBook for free. Just see below in the grey panel where to find your free content and then scan the QR code at the bottom of this page.

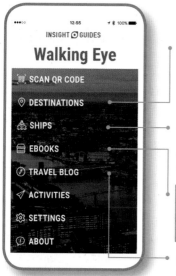

Destinations: Download essential destination content featuring recommended sights and attractions, restaurants, hotels and an A–Z of practical information, all available for purchase.

Ships: Interested in ship reviews? Find independent reviews of river and ocean ships in this section, all available for purchase.

eBooks: You can download your free accompanying digital version of this guide here. You will also find a whole range of other eBooks, all available for purchase.

Free access to travel-related blog articles about different destinations, updated on a daily basis.

HOW THE EBOOKS WORK

The eBooks are provided in EPUB file format. Please note that you will need an eBook reader installed on your device to open the file. Many devices come with this as standard, but you may still need to install one manually from Google Play.

The eBook content is identical to the content in the printed guide.

HOW TO DOWNLOAD THE WALKING EYE APP

1. Download the Walking Eye App from the App Store or Google Play.
2. Open the app and select the scanning function from the main menu.
3. Scan the QR code on this page – you will then be asked a security question to verify ownership of the book.
4. Once this has been verified, you will see your eBook in the purchased ebook section, where you will be able to download it.

Other destination apps and eBooks are available for purchase separately or are free with the purchase of the Insight Guide book.

CONTENTS

CHILDREN

Visit Kelly Tarlton's aquarium (route 2), discover Kiwi wildlife at Rainbow Springs in Rotorua (route 6) and look out for seals in the Wairarapa region (route 9).

RECOMMENDED ROUTES FOR...

DAREDEVILS

Try rafting waterfalls around Rotorua (route 5), glacier hiking and ice-climbing on the Franz Josef and Fox glaciers (route 15) or bungy-jumping where the craze originated, near Queenstown (route 16 and route 17).

FOOD AND WINE

Enjoy a vineyard tour at Martinborough, the heart of the Marlborough wine industry (route 9), in the Waipara Valley wine region (route 13) or in Gibbston Valley (route 17), near Queenstown.

GEOTHERMAL ACTIVITY

For spouting geysers, bubbling mud pools and natural hot springs, visit Rotorua (route 6) or Taupo (route 7).

HISTORY HUNTERS

Retrace the past at Auckland's War Memorial Museum (route 1), at Waitangi, home to modern New Zealand's founding document (route 3), and at the Museum of New Zealand in Wellington (route 8).

PAMPERING

Luxuriate in your own freshly dug pool on Hot Water Beach (route 4), at Rotorua's Polynesian Spa (route 6), in hot saltwater near Mount Maunganui (route 5) and at Hanmer Springs Thermal Resort and Spa (route 13).

SPORTY TYPES

Try yachting or watch the All Blacks in Auckland (route 1), join in the 'Round the Bays' run (route 2), hike up Flagstaff Hill in the Bay of Islands (route 3) or go surfing near Whangamata (route 4).

UNBEATABLE VIEWS

New Zealand boasts many amazing vistas: highlights include the views around Aoraki/Mount Cook (route 14), the scenery around the Franz Josef and Fox glaciers (route 15) and the spectacle of Milford Sound (route 18).

INTRODUCTION

An introduction to New Zealand's geography, customs and culture, plus illuminating background information on cuisine, history and what to do when you're there.

Rere Falls, near Gisborne, in the East Cape

EXPLORE NEW ZEALAND

New Zealand's archipelago of around 700 islands offers a wealth of dramatic scenery, from the exquisite beauty of the Southern Alps and Milford Sound, to the solitude of Lake Waikaremoana and the bubbling surprises of the thermal regions.

New Zealand is situated in the South Pacific between latitudes 34° and 47° South. It's a long, narrow country with two main islands – prosaically known as North Island and South Island – separated by the Cook Strait. The Pacific Ocean crashes into its east coast and the Tasman Sea laps against its western shore. At 269,057 sq km (103,883 sq miles), it's slightly larger than the British Isles. Two-thirds of the country is mountainous and dissected by swift-flowing rivers, deep alpine lakes and subtropical forest. Its highest mountain is Aoraki/ Mount Cook, located in the Southern Alps, which run like a spine down the South Island.

New Zealand was once a remote end-of-the-world gem, loved by the adventurous few who got this far and were astounded at the riches they found packed into a small country. This abruptly changed in 2001, with *The Lord of the Rings: The Fellowship of the Ring*, directed by native son Peter Jackson. Cast in the role of Middle Earth, New Zealand's spectacular landscapes became the southern hemisphere's worst-kept secret.

GETTING AROUND

For the independent traveller, New Zealand's geography can present challenges. The country's length and rough-hewn nature, plus its division into two main islands, make travel time-consuming. The routes in this book focus on five main hubs – Auckland, Rotorua, Wellington, Christchurch and Queenstown – with a number of additional routes guiding you around the rest of the country's attractions (the historic Bay of Islands, the beautiful beaches of Coromandel Peninsula, the adventure activities around Lake Taupo, the wineries of Wairarapa, the stunning glaciers of the South Island's west coast, and the majesty of Milford Sound). If time allows, the routes can be linked together for an exploration of the whole country. If time is at a premium, use domestic flights to travel between the city hubs, then hire a car to access regional attractions.

NORTH ISLAND

Auckland and Northland
In subtropical Northland, proud forests of majestic kauri trees, some thousands

South Bay, Kaikoura

Sunset over Auckland

of years old, stand sentinel. Gnarled red-blossoming pohutukawa trees (known as New Zealand Christmas trees) cling to windswept cliffs over golden beaches, and green rolling hills of farmland span from coast to coast. Thermal activity abounds – there's Auckland, built on extinct volcanoes; Rotorua, famous for its intense thermal activity in the form of geysers, hot springs and pools of boiling mud; and one of New Zealand's most special experiences: digging your own warm spa in the sand at Coromandel's Hot Water Beach (see page 46).

Lake Taupo and Wellington

At the heart of the North Island lies Lake Taupo (see page 58), New Zealand's largest lake: a huge volcanic crater fed by the mountains of the Central Plateau. Hidden beneath hills beside a crater-formed harbour, the capital city of Wellington is the departure point to the magnificent South Island.

SOUTH ISLAND

The South Island provides travellers with an awe-inspiring panorama of majestic snowy mountains, dripping rainforest, silent fiords, sensational sounds, ancient glaciers, wide-open plains and sparkling blue lakes and rivers. Home to only one quarter of the country's population, this is a place of grandeur and solitude. The sensational Southern Alps, a range of jagged peaks running the length of the South Island, were formed by a collision of tectonic plates, which continue to force the mountains upwards by some 10mm per year. Aoraki/Mount Cook, New Zealand's highest mountain, dominates the range at 3,750 metres (12,303ft).

West coast

Home to dense forests of beech, deep fiords, the icy tongues of Franz Josef and Fox glaciers (see page 92), and the picturesque lakeside townships of Wanaka, Queenstown and Te Anau, all vibrant centres for outdoor adventure.

East coast

Christchurch has been gradually recovering from the devastating earthquakes of 2010 and 2011. The resilience and creativity of the city's population is inspirational as they rebuild their home from the rubble left after the quake floored over 70 percent of the CBD's buildings. It may not yet be as beautiful as it once was, but Christchurch has a vibrancy that makes it well worth a visit.

GEOLOGY

New Zealand's separation from other landmasses about 100 million years ago allowed many ancient plants and animals to survive and evolve in isolation. For this reason its landscape features an unrivalled variety of landforms, as well as unique flora and fauna. In a couple of days' driving it is possible to see everything from mountain ranges and

Morning surf time at Kaikoura

sandy beaches to lush rainforests, active volcanoes, glaciers, sounds and fiords.

CLIMATE AND SEASONS

New Zealand's climate ranges from subtropical in Northland to temperate and cool in the deep south. Places such as Invercargill, on the southern coast of the South Island, can be bitterly cold in winter when southerly winds blow up from Antarctica. Summer runs from December to February, autumn from March to May, winter from June to August, and spring from September to November.

Clothing
Whatever the season, be prepared for anything. A typical day in Auckland alternates wildly between showers and sunshine. In the South Island, Fiordland and the West Coast have very high rainfall – Milford Sound gets over 6 metres (20ft) of rain a year.

Alpine weather is notoriously changeable – if you're planning to visit mountainous regions, bring plenty of warm clothing, even in summer. Take broken-in walking boots if you intend to do any hiking. Dress is tidy but casual, although some pubs and bars frown on jeans, jandals (flip-flops) and bare feet.

ACTIVITIES

Given New Zealand's diverse, remarkable terrain, and the fact that it has no poisonous critters, it's not surprising that outdoor activities are huge here. Following is a brief description of the main ones; for more information, visit the Tourism New Zealand website: www.newzealand.com.

Bungy-jumping and skydiving
Bungy-jumping began here, and you can still throw yourself off a ledge with a rubber band attached to your ankles at many spectacular locations across the country. If that sounds too passé for you, how about a tandem skydive? The bonus with this thrill is the stunning view offered by the plane ride as you circle up to the drop zone.

Fishing
New Zealand's waters are a breeding ground for a variety of native and introduced fish species, notably trout and salmon, as well as big game. Hire a guide or go it alone – but remember you may need a license for freshwater fishing. Angling shops can provide good advice.

Swimming with dolphins and whale spotting
You can get up close and personal with dolphins at several locations around the country, by hopping aboard a boat tour. Whale-watching tours are available in Kaikoura (see page 72).

Jetboating and rafting
Jetboating – developed here, to cope

Cycling on Te Mata Peak   *A whale-watching trip*

with the country's swift-flowing and broad, shallow rivers – is now a source of white-knuckle fun. Visitors can hop aboard for thrilling high-speed rides at several locations nationwide.

A fantastic – and even more immersive – way to experience New Zealand's fast-flowing rivers is in a raft. Rivers range from grade 1 (easy) to grade 5 (extreme), and trips vary from a few hours to a few days.

Snowsports
New Zealand's rugged terrain offers a wide range of skiing in winter. North Island's commercial ski fields include Whakapapa and Turoa, both on the slopes of Mount Ruapehu, while in the

---

DON'T LEAVE NEW ZEALAND WITHOUT...

Seeing a real live kiwi. The unofficial national symbol of New Zealand, kiwis are only active at night and are hard to spot in the wild – but you're assured a sighting at the Kiwi Encounter at Rainbow Springs in Rotorua. See page 52.

Getting into rugby. Sport in New Zealand is synonymous with rugby and the national team, the All Blacks. If you can't see a game in Auckland, check out the New Zealand Sports Hall of Fame in Dunedin. See page 74.

Watching a volcano erupt. White Island in the Bay of Plenty continuously discharges gas so pressurised it roars like a squadron of B52 bombers. This is the only place in the world where you can see an active marine volcano close up. See page 48.

Visiting a Maori village. In the Rotorua forest you can visit Tamaki Maori Village, where local guides introduce Maori culture, myths and legends, and song and dance. After a traditional meal, end the evening with a *hongi* – a pressing of noses to signify friendship. See page 51.

Searching for the Ring. The Queenstown region stars in numerous scenes in the *Hobbit* and *Lord of the Rings* movies. To take a tour see www.trilogytrail.com.

Hitting the slopes. Between June and October, New Zealand's highlands are a winter wonderland. Try Whakapapa and ski down a volcano on Mount Ruapehu near Lake Taupo on the North Island, or explore the South Island's nine commercial ski fields. See pages 60 and 87.

Going wild and getting wet. Whether it's sailing in Auckland, taking a white-knuckle trip down the Shotover River or experiencing a fast and furious excursion to the Hole in the Rock in the Bay of Islands, you can't leave New Zealand without getting on the water. See pages 35, 96 and 39.

Enjoying a local glass. New Zealand produces some of the best wine in the world. Go sipping at the source at vineyards in the Wairarapa, Marlborough and Canterbury regions. See page 68.

Taking the plunge. Bungy-jumping was invented here. Test your mettle at one of the classic jump sites in Lake Taupo or Queenstown. See page 82.

Wellington local

South Island Queenstown offers a range of fields within easy reach, as does the city of Christchurch.

LANGUAGE

New Zealand has two official languages: English and Maori. Nearly everyone speaks English (with a distinctive, often nasal, accent). New Zealand has adopted standard English grammar and spelling, but has also added some 'Kiwi-isms' to the vocabulary. You may hear, for instance, words like 'tramping' (hiking), 'chilly bin' (a portable cooler used for picnics) or 'grog' (alcohol).

Maori

Maori is a language undergoing a renaissance. It's taught in schools and is commonly spoken as a first language in several parts of the North Island. Maori influence is strong throughout the country in place names, and many words have entered common usage, for example: *Pakeha*, meaning a person of European descent; *kia ora*, for hello; *kai*, for food; *koha*, if a donation is required; and *hangi*, a style of Maori cooking.

Pronunciation isn't difficult once you master the vowels, which often occur alongside each other but are pronounced separately: a as in 'car'; e as in 'men'; i like 'ea' in 'bean'; o like 'aw' in 'paw'; u like 'oo' in 'moon'. The only complex sounds are wh, pronounced more or less like 'f', and ng, pronounced like the 'ng' in 'singing'. Syllables are given equal stress. Maori words do not take an 's' to form the plural.

The ultimate linguistic test

If you feel you've gained a certain proficiency in the Maori language, try one of the longest place names in the world, attached to a hill in the Hawke's Bay area. In its shortened version it's called Taumatawhakatangihangakoauauotamateapokaiwhenuakitanatahu. It means, 'Where Tamatea of the big knees, the man who slid down, climbed and consumed mountains and is known as the land-eater, played the flute to his beloved'.

GOVERNMENT

New Zealand is a sovereign, independent democratic state and a member of both the United Nations and the Commonwealth. The government is elected every three years under the proportional representation system called MMP. The Government's leader is the Prime Minister, while the Head of State is the Queen of England, who is represented here by a resident Governor-General.

Green philosophy

The Maori story of creation explains that land and human beings are all one – flesh and clay from the same source material. The indigenous Maori's emotional attachment to place is profound

Polynesian culture celebrated

and has influenced *Pakeha* (European) culture, contributing to the national belief that 'clean and green' is a genuine philosophy, not a marketing slogan.

TOP TIPS FOR VISITING NEW ZEALAND

Local customs. New Zealand's custom officials are extremely strict about what they do and do not let into the country. Don't be surprised if your walking boots or tent are taken off for a scrub, and be careful not to inadvertently leave fruit or other food in your pockets or bag when you arrive – fines can be stiff and tolerance is low.

Plan for greatness. If you plan on hiking any of New Zealand's Great Walks (nine trekking routes identified as the country's best – see www.newzealand.com for more), plan and book ahead – the number of trampers on these routes is regulated, and the allocation quickly fills up in the warmer months.

A word on birds. When in mountainous areas, beware of the winged hooligans otherwise known as keas – alpine parrots with no fear of humans and zero respect for property, who will stop at nothing to get your food.

Once bitten. In certain areas, such as Milford Sound and Fiordland in general, sandflies are a major annoyance. When the sandflies go to bed, mosquitoes often come out to party. Take plenty of insect repellent, light long-sleeve garments and, if you intend spending a lot of time outdoors, consider hat nets.

Breathe easy. When driving in New Zealand, it's now illegal to have a blood alcohol content of more than 0.05 percent for those over 20 years old, and 0.03 percent for those under 20. There is a low tolerance of overstepping these limits, so the advice is not to drink and drive at all.

Find your wings. It might seem like an extravagance, but if you're going to try flightseeing anywhere, New Zealand in the place to splurge – particularly over the magnificent Southern Alps – and it might not be as expensive as you think. Flights over Aoraki/Mount Cook and the glaciers with Lake Tekapo's Air Safaris (www.airsafaris.co.nz), for example, cost from NZ$340.

Arrive alive. While New Zealand has some fantastic driving routes and the roads are generally good, the country has a relatively high rate of road deaths. In country areas roads can be twisty and/or icy, and journeys can be long. Take regular rests on big trips, stick to speed limits and always carry chains during colder months (it's illegal not to carry chains on some routes – such as the Milford Road – during winter).

Be prepared. New Zealand's weather is dictated by the country's wild mountainous terrain and exposed position in the Southern Ocean, and it can be unpredictable. The best approach is to take layers of warm and waterproof clothing, which can be taken off or put on according to changing conditions.

New Zealand lamb

FOOD AND DRINK

Kiwi cooking is distinguished by a style that fuses influences, reflecting the country's cultural diversity. A latecomer to the world of wine making, it now also produces outstanding vintages that are sold and acclaimed worldwide.

Fresh and vibrant, New Zealand's cuisine is often described as Pacific Rim. It draws much inspiration from Europe, Asia and Polynesia, and this blend of influences has created a mouth-watering range of flavours and food that can be sampled in cafés, restaurants and lodges nationwide. Innovative chefs make clever use of tasty ingredients freshly harvested from the garden, land and sea – which, in the company of award-winning local wines, make the New Zealand gastronomic experience among the best in the world.

While food and beverage production has long been the linchpin of New Zealand's prosperity and a leading export earner, it's the fusion of unique, quality produce and ethnic influences that has allowed a national food identity to evolve. Nowadays New Zealand's worldwide reputation for award-winning produce draws visitors from afar to the source, and food tourism is developing at a rapid rate.

TRADITIONAL DINING

The country's food culture is also distinctive in the way that New Zealanders prefer to eat in an environment that is as relaxed and unaffected as possible, in tune with the laid-back Kiwi psyche. Summer usually means endless barbecues and alfresco dining, with the emphasis on fresh, simple fare, organic or home-grown produce, and indigenous foods. Fare such as lamb, venison and fish – including crayfish (lobster) and other shellfish such as pipi, tuatua and scallops – are staples.

The hangi

For an authentic New Zealand eating experience, try a traditional Maori *hangi* (pronounced 'hung-ee'), cooked underground. A deep hole is dug, then lined with red-hot stones and covered with vegetation. The food (chicken, pork, lamb, potatoes, kumara – sweet potato – and other vegetables) is placed on top, then the whole 'oven' is sprinkled with water, sealed and left to steam for several hours, giving the food a smoky taste.

Traditionally, all members of a *whanau* (family) come for the feast, with stereotypical gender roles the norm: the men digging and working on the hole, and the women preparing the food to go in it. Several tourist locations, including Rotorua in the North Island, invite visitors to

Green-lipped mussels

Nin's Bin has been selling crayfish since the 1970s

join in and experience *hangi* culture (see page 53).

SEAFOOD

Fish is abundant and excellent in New Zealand, with varieties including freshwater salmon, sole and flounder. If you want to eat trout, however, note that you will have to catch your own, as it is illegal to sell it. A seasonal delicacy is *inanga* (whitebait), a tiny minnow-like fish that can be enjoyed nationwide, although it has become synonymous with the South Island's West Coast.

On your travels, look out for roadside stalls selling succulent crayfish and/or freshly smoked mussels or fish. The sublime flavour of crayfish can also be enjoyed at any good seafood restaurant; try White Morph (Kaikoura, South Island) or Harbourside Seafood Bar & Grill (Quay Street, Auckland).

Throughout the year, shellfish such as mussels, pipi and tuatua can be gathered freely from the beach. Green-lipped mussels, *paua* (abalone) and oysters – the Pacific oyster, the rock oyster and the famed Bluff oyster – can also be found on menus nationwide.

NATIONAL SPECIALITIES

Your New Zealand culinary experience is incomplete until you savour the sweet, creamy stickiness of pavlova, the national dessert. In addition, it's worth looking out for some food products that offer an entirely new taste sensation. These include hokey pokey ice cream (vanilla ice cream with toffee bits in it), L&P soft drink (short for 'Lemon and Paeroa', a lemon-on-flavoured sparkling drink), tamarillos (tree tomatoes), feigoas (a fruit), pineapple lumps (chocolate-covered pineapple chews) and chocolate fish.

To discover more about New Zealand cuisine, you can also learn to cook the Kiwi way from an expert. Cooking classes are becoming popular, with courses including Ruth Pretty's Cooking School (www.ruthpretty.co.nz) in Te Horo, north of Wellington, which attract foodies from far and wide.

Indigenous treats include kumara, a type of sweet potato and an essential part of any Sunday roast, Rewena and Takakau bread, piko piko pesto, and huhu grubs – the latter found in backyards nationwide, but usually only served at local wild foods festivals.

FOOD FESTIVALS

Food festivals are regularly held throughout the nation, but when it comes to wild cuisine, there's no better place to start than Hokitika. This West Coast town leads the way in untamed gastronomic creativity, with all manner of culinary delights up for grabs during the annual Wild Foods Festival, held to celebrate the harvest.

Stallholders provide crowds with a variety of bizarre tucker, from crickets and huhu grubs to bull's penis and pig's ears

Fresh, light food is fashionable

and even worm sushi. The less adventurous are not forgotten, however, with gourmet treats such as rabbit pâté, pickled seaweed, ostrich pie, crayfish, whitebait and home-made ice cream also available. Wine and food festivals are held annually in Auckland, Bay of Islands, Coromandel, Hawke's Bay, Martinborough, Blenheim, Canterbury and Queenstown. These national and regional events highlight the production of a wide-ranging supply of gourmet foods and boutique wines.

WINE

Needless to say, New Zealand wines are the only complement to the local cuisine that visitors should consider during their stay. It all began at the top of the country in the Bay of Islands, with James Busby, official British Resident, horticulturist extraordinaire, pioneer viticulturist (he also founded the wine industry in New South Wales, Australia) and author of the *Treaty of Waitangi*. He planted the first vineyard on his property at Waitangi

in the Bay of Islands in 1833, and a couple of years later the very first New Zealand wine was produced.

From that point forward the history of wine-making in New Zealand becomes obscure. However, it is known that early French settlers planted small vineyards at Akaroa (South Island) and Marist Brothers established a winery at Mission Estate (www.missionestate.co.nz) in Hawke's Bay in 1865. This is still operating and is now a commercial venture, making it New Zealand's oldest vineyard.

By the end of the century, small commercial vineyards were established in other parts of Hawke's Bay and in the Auckland-Northland region. However, vineyards countrywide suffered and the wine industry was effectively destroyed by prohibition politics between 1900 and 1920. Fortunately the industry is now thriving with several distinct wine-growing regions, each with its own wine trail. Many vineyards offer a cellar door experience.

International standing

If New Zealand has a signature wine, it's sauvignon blanc, but pinot noir is also in the running. To sample fruity, fresh-scented sauvignon blancs from a range of award-winning vineyards, head to the notoriously sunny valleys of the Marlborough region (www.wine-marlborough.co.nz). Pinot noir has placed the southern North Island wine-growing region of the Wairarapa (www.wairarapanz.com) firmly on the map, and other varietals including syrah (known in Australia and

---

Food and drink prices

Throughout this guide, we have used the following price ranges to denote the approximate cost of a two-course meal for one with a glass of house wine:

$$$$ = above NZ$80
$$$ = NZ$60–80
$$ = NZ$40–60
$ = below NZ$40

On the Hawke's Bay wine trail   *Dining alfresco at Huka Lodge*

New Zealand as shiraz) and pinot gris are steadily increasing in popularity.

BEER

Beer is perennially popular throughout New Zealand. In pubs it is often sold in pint glasses or a 'handle', but measures vary much more than they do in the UK (a 'pint' can mean anything from 425ml – the Kiwi standard – to the traditional British 568ml imperial measure).

Boutique breweries and craft ales have experienced a revolution in recent years, and beer lovers will now find far more choice when they go to the bar and the 'bottle shop' than the usual old suspects such as DB and Speights.

The produce of independent brewing companies – such as Wellington's brilliantly named Yeastie Boys – can be found all over the country. For an excellent map showing microbreweries and craft-beer pubs, visit www.beertourist.co.nz.

WHERE TO EAT

Most major towns and cities have a range of eateries, from food courts to cafés, casual restaurants and brasseries, through to high-class establishments. Wellington has more food haunts per capita than New York City, with over 300 cafés and restaurants doing business within the 2km (1.25-mile) radius of its inner city.

Like everything, you will get what you pay for, but it's fair to say that there is a trend towards a lighter and healthier style of cooking, with a focus on fresh New Zealand produce. Likewise, cafés are increasingly replacing the tearooms of old. Most restaurants/cafés offer at least one or two vegetarian and/or gluten-free dishes on their menu.

Cafés open as early as 7am, while most restaurants tend to commence service around 6pm, with last orders taken around 10pm. Note that in smaller towns it's best to book, as restaurants will close early – or not open at all – if they think they have no patrons. Many restaurants are licensed, and BYO (Bring Your Own) places – licensed for the consumption but not the sale of alcohol – are also popular. Some licensed restaurants also offer BYO, but typically charge a 'corkage' fee.

SHOPPING FOR FOOD

Supermarkets with a huge selection of produce from around the world are common in the larger towns and cities, as are delis and boutique bakeries, while more regional areas will usually have a local convenience shop, or 'milk bar' (corner store selling essentials, papers and sweets/candies/lollies). Many New Zealanders do part of their main weekly shop at their local farmers' market, making the most of reasonably priced seasonal produce and home-made preserves. Hand-made cheeses, artisan breads, natural ice cream, hand-crafted chocolates, gourmet meats and organic coffee are also often up for grabs.

Find handmade pottery

SHOPPING

Trade in your New Zealand dollars for, among other things, hand-crafted Maori carvings, pretty jade and iridescent paua-shell jewellery, hand-made pottery and, of course, woolly jumpers and sheepskin goods.

New Zealand offers a huge variety of shopping, from arts and craft markets, gallery and museum shops to exclusive designer stores. For traditional souvenirs, look for hand-crafted Maori carvings in wood, bone and *pounamu* (greenstone or jade). You can also find jewellery and ornaments made from the iridescent *paua* shell (abalone). New Zealand potters are among the world's finest, and today many artisans are also working in stone, wood, glass and metals. With over 40 million sheep, it is no surprise that the country's wool industry is going strong; wonderful hand-knitted wool sweaters, beautiful wall hangings, homespun yarns and top-quality sheepskins are plentiful. New Zealand also has 70 million feral possums, so expect to see possum-skin goods, too. Alongside top international fashion labels in the main urban areas, you will also find New Zealand's own fashion labels, including Zambesi, NomD, Karen Walker and World.

Kiwis also love the outdoors, and they have developed a wide range of hard-wearing clothing and equipment to match the tough environment. Warm and rugged farm-wear such as Swanndri bush shirts and jackets are popular purchases, while mountaineering equipment, camping gear and backpacks set world standards. Some items have even become fashion success stories, such as the Canterbury range of rugby and yachting jerseys, and the Icebreaker brand of fashionable merino wear.

The majority of shops and businesses open 9am to 5pm, Monday to Friday, but many stores also open on Saturday and Sunday, especially in the large cities. In resort areas, too, you will find shops open in the evenings, until around 9pm.

Most shops accept major debit and credit cards, including Visa and Mastercard. American Express is less widely accepted. Some smaller stores may not be set up for contactless transactions, however.

WHERE TO BUY

Auckland
New Zealand's largest city offers some of the country's most varied retail therapy. Queen Street is the hub for souvenir shopping, with 'downtown' Queen Street hosting the major duty-free stores. For a full range of items, try the DFS Galleria on the corner of Customs Street and Albert

Auckland's Queen Street   *Handcrafted jewellery for sale*

Street. Vulcan Lane, off Queen Street, leads to High Street and the Chancery District, where Auckland's major designer fashion boutiques are clustered. The wares of up-and-coming designers can be found in the city fringe suburbs of Ponsonby and Parnell. For something different, visit the Devonport Craft Market (32 Clarence Street, Devonport; www.devonportcraftmarket.blogspot.com; last Sunday of every month).

Rotorua

The main shopping street in Rotorua is Tutanekai Street, although several souvenir shops are on Fenton Street, close to the Visitor Centre. Maori arts and crafts abound here, as do leather and sheepskin products. The Best of Maori Tourism (1189 Fenton Street) offers original Maori-designed clothing and carvings in bone and wood. Craftspeople can be watched while they work at The Jade Factory (1288 Fenton Street), and at Te Puia, the New Zealand Maori Arts and Crafts Institute at Whakarewarewa on Hemo Road.

Wellington

Wellington's shopping scene is second to none. Designer names to look out for include Karen Walker, Zambesi and local Wellingtonians Mandatory, Starfish, Voon and Andrea Moore. Shopping in the capital city centres around Lambton Quay and ranges from high-street chains such as Farmers, to clothing chain stores such as Country Road and Max. David Jones, a large department store in the former Kirkaldie and Staines premises on Lambton Quay, offers a mix of New Zealand, Australian and international brands. For crafts and antiques, spend an hour or two browsing the converted villas of Tinakori Road. For less mainstream fashions, try the small designer clothing stores that compete for space with second-hand bookshops along Cuba Street.

Christchurch

Ballantyne's, the city's iconic department store on Cashel Street, has Kiwi designers such as Trelise Cooper, Kate Sylvester and Huffer, alongside well-known international clothing brands. Nearby, The Crossing Shopping Centre opened to great fanfare in 2017 and is home to an expanding number of international fashion and homeware stores. Away from the CBD, The Tannery in Woolston houses boutique shops in a tastefully converted 19th-century building.

Queenstown

Jewellery, duty-free and artisan stores line The Mall, while O'Connells Shopping Centre, at the corner of Camp Street and Beach Street, hosts around 25 stores under one roof, including New Zealand's largest Canterbury of New Zealand store. It sells a wide range of All Blacks and rugby-inspired clothing. Queenstown's focus on outdoor pursuits is strongly reflected in its wealth of high-quality sportswear apparel and equipment shops, which can be found all over town. Many stores open for extended hours on a daily basis.

Performing the traditional Maori war cry dance, the Haka

ENTERTAINMENT

In the past, many Kiwis found it necessary to relocate overseas to get their talents seen and move their careers forward; not so these days. Those who have made it big at home have inspired a whole new level of confidence in Kiwi creativity.

New Zealand's arts landscape has been formed by a blend of influences, a kaleidoscope of Maori, Samoan, Pacific Island, European and Asian cultures. From film-makers and performers, to writers, designers and musicians, each has helped to evolve New Zealand's performing arts scene, which is incredibly strong for a small Pacific Island nation with limited funding.

THEATRE

Maori and Pacific Island writers and performers have provided New Zealand's theatre with a unique and colourful Polynesian-influenced identity. Theatre companies such as Wellington's Taki Rua (www.takirua.co.nz) and the Auckland Theatre Company (www.atc.co.nz) both stage local plays. The Court Theatre in Christchurch (www.courttheatre.org.nz) is regarded as New Zealand's leading theatre, with a small, high-quality ensemble; it relocated to 'the Shed' in the suburb of Addington after the Christchurch Arts Centre was badly damaged in the 2011 earthquake. Smaller venues producing edgier works in Auckland include Silo (www.

silotheatre.co.nz) and Depot Arts Space (www.depotartspace.co.nz). Daring and inspired works can be seen at Wellington's Bats (www.bats.co.nz).

DANCE

Dance has always played a major role in Maori culture and Kapa Haka (performance dances) is an integral part of daily life in New Zealand; the best groups tour internationally to share this unique form of cultural art.

The Royal New Zealand Ballet is well worth seeing, along with a plethora of contemporary dance companies including Auckland's Black Grace Dance Company which performs worldwide, and Wellington's Footnote Dance Company. Auckland's all-male dance company, Black Grace, features some of New Zealand's most respected contemporary dancers (www.blackgrace.co.nz).

MUSIC

In 2013, teenage singer songwriter Lorde (real name Ella Marija Lani Yelich-O'Connor) burst onto international airwaves with her brilliantly precocious

Classic cars at Napier's Art Deco Weekend

anthem *Royals*, which won two Grammy Awards. Her subsequent album *Pure Heroine* was highly acclaimed. Other exciting Kiwi acts include Ladyhawke, the Datsuns and the Mint Chicks, while Crowded House's Neil Finn remains the country's best-known senior musician. Musical comedy duo, the Flight of the Conchords, were another huge success story in recent years.

New Zealand has three professional symphony orchestras, including the New Zealand Symphony Orchestra (NZSO), and several choirs including the National Youth Choir, which regularly wins international events. Recent co-productions between the Royal New Zealand Ballet, NZSO, and Maori music and dance groups have showcased New Zealand's contemporary bi-cultural 'fusion'. Meanwhile, the modern and alternative music scene is diverse and vibrant in New Zealand.

FILM

Building upon cultural icon Peter Jackson's *Lord of the Rings* trilogy and the later production of the epic story's prequel, *The Hobbit*, indigenous film projects have, in recent times, been hugely successful. Director Nicky Caro followed her international hit *Whale Rider* with *In My Father's Den*, a favourite at international film festivals. Other New Zealand directors turning heads include Taika Waititi (*Two Cars, One Night*) and Andrew Adamson (*Prince Caspian*). It's

fitting that Peter Jackson's home town of Wellington has more screens per capita than anywhere else in New Zealand; among these is The Embassy Theatre, the city's grandest.

NIGHTLIFE

New Zealand's nightlife is, by international standards, limited, and really only exists in major cities. Most small towns boast only a pub but main cities offer a variety of dance clubs, live music venues and late-night bars. To find out what's on, check the entertainment pages of local newspapers or visit www.eventfindaer.co.nz, a site dedicated to New Zealand culture online. You can book on this site by following the links, or alternatively, most major events can be booked through Ticketek (www.ticketek.co.nz). Other publications that list entertainment details include *Rip it Up*.

FESTIVALS

While New Zealand's nightlife may be tame, its festivals are rather wacky. Highlights include The World of Wearable Art Awards in Wellington; Christchurch's World Buskers Festival; Hokitika's Wild Foods Festival; Napier's Art Deco Weekend and Taihape's Gumboot Day. However, the most significant celebration is Waitangi Day, when the signing of New Zealand's founding document, the *Treaty of Waitangi*, is celebrated nationwide.

At the Treaty of Waitanga, Maori chiefs ceded sovereignty to the British crown

HISTORY: KEY DATES

From early days as a Polynesian settlement and the arrival of the Maori to European rule and, finally, independence, the list below covers important social and political events in the history of New Zealand.

DISCOVERY

800	First Polynesian settlers arrive.
1642	Abel Tasman becomes first known European to 'discover' New Zealand.
1645	Dutch cartographers name the land Nova Zeelandia after the Dutch province of Zeeland.
1769	Captain James Cook explores New Zealand.

19TH CENTURY

1814	Reverend Samuel Marsden establishes Anglican mission station.
1826	Attempt at European settlement under Captain Herd.
1840	Treaty of Waitangi is signed by 50 Maori chiefs. Arrival of New Zealand Company's settlers in Wellington.
1841	New Zealand proclaimed independent of New South Wales.
1844	'Northern War' between Maori and *Pakeha* (Europeans).
1852	Constitution Act passed. New Zealand is divided into six provinces.
1853	The Maori King movement, designed to protect tribal land, begins.
1854	First session of the General Assembly in Auckland.
1860	The first 'Taranaki War' begins between the government and Maori over land ownership.
1861	Gold discovery in Otago. First electric telegraph line opens.
1865	Seat of government transferred to Wellington from Auckland.
1867	Maori are given the vote.
1870	New Zealand's first rugby match. Last battles of 'New Zealand Wars'.
1876	Provincial governments abolished.
1893	Universal female suffrage is introduced.

The 2011 earthquake in Christchurch caused immense damage

20TH CENTURY

1907	The country is granted Dominion status.
1914–18	World War I. Gallipoli campaign by ANZAC troops.
1931	Hawke's Bay earthquake.
1935	First New Government elected (Labour).
1939–45	World War II. New Zealand Division serves in Italy.
1951	Prolonged waterfront industrial dispute. New Zealand signs ANZUS Treaty alliance with US and Australia.
1953	Sir Edmund Hillary successfully climbs Mount Everest.
1974	Christchurch hosts the Commonwealth Games.
1975	Waitangi Tribunal established to hear Maori land-rights issues. National Party elected.
1981	Tour of New Zealand by South African rugby team leads to riots.
1983	Closer Economic Relations (CER) agreement with Australia.
1984	New Zealand becomes nuclear-free.
1985	Greenpeace protest vessel *Rainbow Warrior* bombed by French agents in Auckland.
1993	Electoral system changed to a proportional system called MMP.
1994	New Zealand wins America's Cup yachting regatta in San Diego.
1995	Waikato's Tainui tribe settles a long-standing grievance claim.
1999	New Zealand hosts APEC summit and America's Cup.

21ST CENTURY

2004	*The Lord of the Rings: The Return of the King* wins all 11 Academy Awards for which it was nominated.
2007	Sir Edmund Hillary passes away. The nation goes into mourning.
2010	Magnitude 7.1 earthquake rocks Christchurch. Pike River Mine disaster claims lives of 29 coal miners.
2011	Shallow magnitude 6.3 earthquake centred in Christchurch claims 185 lives. New Zealand hosts Rugby World Cup.
2014	New Zealand's National party win a third term in government.
2016	Bill English is elected leader of the National Party and Prime Minister after Key's unexpected resignation. A series of powerful (7.8-magnitude) earthquakes strike South Island, leaving two people dead.
2017	Following a close-run election, Labour forms a coalition with the populist New Zealand First party, with Green Party support.

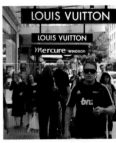

BEST ROUTES

The city by night

AUCKLAND

The country's largest city sits between the harbours of Waitemata and Manukau on an isthmus dotted with extinct volcanoes. This walking tour takes in its key sights, including Auckland Domain, Parnell and the Sky Tower.

DISTANCE: 7km (4.5 miles)
TIME: A full day
START: Viaduct Harbour
END: Sky Tower
POINTS TO NOTE: There is much ground to cover on this route – you can take bus or taxi rides between key points of interest to spare your feet and save some time. Another option is to board the Auckland Explorer Bus (www.explorerbus.co.nz; charge), a hop-on/hop-off tour featuring many of the sights on this and the next route. Tours depart from the Ferry Building on Quay Street.

Sandwiched between twin harbours and built on 53 extinct volcanoes, Auckland has long been New Zealand's major gateway and largest city. Almost 1.5 million people call Auckland home, and they are a vibrant and diverse bunch. It has the biggest Polynesian population of any city in the world and boasts a large Asian community. Several scenic areas – such as the Waitakere Ranges to the west, the Hunua Ranges to the south, and Waiwera and Puhoi to the north – have been maintained as greenbelt areas and protected from development.

City of Sails

West of Auckland are the shallow waters of Manukau Harbour, navigable only by small ships. Waitemata Harbour to the east is a 'Sea of Sparkling Water', indented with bays and scattered with islands. One of them, Rangitoto, an active volcano until 200 years ago, stands guard at the harbour entrance.

To the Maori, the area was *Tamaki Makaurau*, 'the place of a hundred lovers'. British administrators renamed it, rather less poetically, after an English admiral and the city is informally known as 'City of Sails'. It's said to possess the highest number of boats per head of population on the planet, and it certainly looks that way each January, during the Anniversary Day yachting regatta, the world's largest one-day sailing event. The race celebrates the foundation of the city in 1840 as capital of

Racing yachts at full speed near Auckland

the country – a title it lost 25 years later to Wellington.

VIADUCT HARBOUR

This tour of the city begins downtown at the **Viaduct Harbour ❶**, where **Mecca**, see ❶, does good breakfasts. After strolling the waterfront, exit the harbour at Quay Street archway, where a large suspended yacht, a legacy of New Zealand's endeavours in the America's Cup regatta, is on display. For a taste of America's Cup action, pop into **Explore**

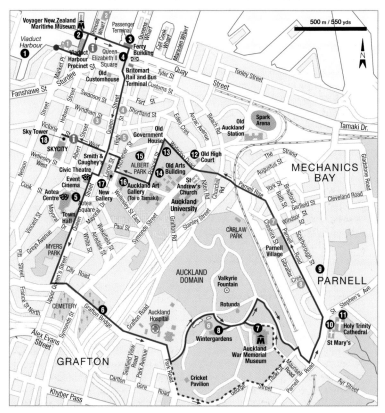

Apartments by Viaduct Harbour

NZ (www.exploregroup.co.nz), which organises thrilling trips aboard *NZL 40* and *NZL 41*.

Auckland's impressive Harbour Bridge took 200 workers around four years to complete, using 6,500 tonnes of concrete and nearly 6,000 tonnes of steel, before it opened on 30 May 1959. For a unique perspective on the city, take a Bridgeclimb (Westhaven Reserve; www.bungy.co.nz/auckland-bridge/auckland-bridge-climbclimb.co.nz; daily; charge), during which you'll be offered a bungy jump on the way down.

Maritime Museum

For an insight into New Zealand's maritime history, check out **Voyager New Zealand Maritime Museum ❷** (Princes Wharf; www.maritimemuseum.co.nz; daily 9am–5pm; charge). The museum showcases boats of all types. After visiting the museum head along the wharf to **Bellini**, see ❷, for a light meal. Boat trips around the harbour aboard the historic steamboat SS *Puke* and the traditional sailing ship SS *Breeze* depart sporadically from here.

Visitor Centre and Ferry Building

From the museum, take a stroll along the waterfront, passing the **i-Site Visitor Centre** (137 Quay Street, Princes Wharf; tel: 09-307 0615; Mon–Fri 8.30am–5.30pm, Sat–Sun 8.30am–5pm) en route to the historic **Ferry Building ❸** at 99 Quay Street. Erected in 1912 to house the offices of harbour

officials, this red-brick edifice is now the focal point for commuter ferries that link Auckland with the North Shore and the islands of the Waitemata Harbour and Hauraki Gulf. (Board from the back of the building.)

QUEEN STREET

Cross Quay Street to the fully paved **Queen Elizabeth II Square ❹**, the home of the Britomart Train Terminus, one of the city's key public transport interchanges and the base of Queen Street, the city's main shopping area. Stroll Queen Street, exploring side streets (home to pit stops including **Revive**, see ❸, and **Café Melba**, see ❹, and eventually leading to the High Street, with boutique and designer stores and the fashionable **Vivace**, see ❺).

Further up on the right you'll pass the department store **Smith & Caughey's** (253–61 Queen Street; www.smithandcaughey.co.nz) and the historic **Civic Theatre** (corner of Queen Street and Wellesley Street; www.civictheatre.co.nz), which hosts many of Auckland's premier events.

AOTEA SQUARE

The adjacent **Aotea Square ❺** has several points of interest. The first is the elaborately carved Maori **Waharoa** (gateway). A symbolic entrance to the square, it stands in stark contrast to the surrounding mirrored-glass buildings.

The view towards the Ferry Building

Across Aotea Square is Auckland's main cultural venue, **Aotea Centre** (www.aucklandlive.co.nz). In the foyer you can find out about current and upcoming events, and purchase tickets. Bordering the square are City Council buildings, including the renovated Town Hall.

Auckland Domain

To get to **Auckland Domain**, New Zealand's oldest park and the ancient site of a huge volcanic explosion, you can walk, catch a bus (the Link bus from Queen Street) or hail a taxi. This journey of about 1km (0.6 mile) will take you over **Grafton Bridge** ❻ and past Auckland Hospital. The wide volcanic crater has formed a natural amphitheatre arching from the hospital to the Auckland War Memorial Museum and is the venue of numerous outdoor sporting and cultural events. If you're on foot, enter via Park Road. If you're travelling by bus, get off on Parnell Road, slightly further southeast.

Auckland War Memorial Museum

The main sight in the park, the imposing **Auckland War Memorial Museum** ❼ (www.aucklandmuseum.com; daily 10am–5pm; charge), enjoys a prime location with panoramic views of the Domain and parts of the city and harbour.

The museum was constructed in 1929 and serves up an excellent overview of the natural, cultural and social history of New Zealand. For the first-time visitor it also provides a superb introduction to Maori culture through its collection of artefacts, including a raised storehouse, a carved meeting house and, possibly the most spectacular exhibit: *Te Toki a Tapiri*, a great Maori war canoe carved from a single totara log. This 25-metre (82ft) -long boat was built in 1836 to seat approximately 100 warriors. There are daily performances featuring traditional Maori song and dance, and the 'Scars on the Heart' display depicts the compelling story of New Zealand at war.

Note the names of locations etched in the stone around the entire museum facade; these were the battlefields where New Zealanders were killed in overseas wars in the 20th century. As you walk around the museum, keep an eye out for Auckland's impressive volcanic peaks. These include **One Tree Hill**, once topped by a lone summit pine but now marked only by an obelisk; **Mount Eden**; and the slopes of **Rangitoto Island**, which last erupted about 600 years ago.

There is a café in the museum, but there's also a treat in store if you walk from the front of the museum back down to the **Wintergarden Cafe**, see ❻. On the south side of the teahouse, a takeaway kiosk (daily 9am–5pm) sells ice creams and other snacks.

If time permits, take a stroll behind the tearooms through the **Wintergardens** ❽ (Apr–Oct daily 9am–4.30pm, Nov–Mar Mon–Sat 9am–5.30pm, Sun 9am–7.30pm; free), a conservatory

Statues in the Wintergardens

housing some 10,000 exotic plants. Look out for the short native bush walk, which gives an indication of the type of vegetation still covering large tracts of the countryside.

PARNELL

From the Wintergardens, follow the path that runs southeast around the perimeter of the Domain and out to Parnell Road. Turn left here and take a 15-minute walk to **Parnell** 🟤, a vibrant inner-city suburb known for its boutique shopping and wide range of eateries.

As you walk, look out on your right, for **St Mary's Church** 🔟, regarded as one of the finest wooden Gothic buildings in New Zealand, and for the **Holy Trinity Cathedral** ⓫, which was only completed in 1995.

Just 30 metres further, at the St Stephen's Avenue intersection, is a mix of bakeries, 'dairies' (small grocery stores), fish-and-chip shops and the start of the designer shops that become more apparent as you venture down the hill. A good pit stop at this point is the **Strawberry Alarm Clock**, see ➆.

The Parnell Village complex on the left-hand side of Parnell Road comprises characterful wooden villas reclaimed and restored for retail purposes. Walk around the verandas and over the little bridges linking villa to villa to access the shops. For lunch and to watch the world go by, get a seat under the awning at **Verve Café**, see ➇.

BACK TO THE CENTRE

After pounding the pavements of Parnell, either hail a taxi or enjoy a half-hour walk back to the city centre. Your ultimate destination, on the corner of Federal and Victoria streets, is the landmark Sky Tower, which offers unparalleled views over the city, the Waitakere Ranges and the gulf islands.

If you're on foot, veer left down Parnell Rise. Once at the bottom, walk under the rail bridge and cross the Grafton motorway extension, then take a deep breath before tackling the hill on the other side. A path leads from Churchill Road up through a reserve area to the junction of Symonds Street and Alten Road, to the Romanesque columns of the Presbyterian **St Andrew's Church**. Directly opposite the church are the lower grounds of **Auckland University**.

Cross over, head west along the Waterloo Quadrant and, on your right, you will see the old **High Court** ⓬, with its historic chamber and courtrooms joined to a modern extension. Work started on the old Court building in 1865, and the first sitting took place three years later. The carved stone heads and gargoyles adorning its exterior were crafted by Anton Teutenburg, a Prussian immigrant who was paid 15 shillings a day for the task.

Moving on, you will see, on the left, at 12 Princes Street, the **Old Government House** ⓭, completed in

The marina

Smart town houses in Parnell

1856 and the former residence of the Governor-General of New Zealand. Cross the road to the entrance and take a stroll through the grounds, now owned by Auckland University. The building appears to be stone but is in fact clad entirely in kauri, a tall coniferous tree that once dominated New Zealand's landscape. Walk alongside the building and enjoy the lush subtropical gardens on the hillside leading up to Princes Street.

Make your way up Princes Street, where on the left you will see the **Old Arts Building** ⓮, designed and built with the help of students from Auckland University College and opened in 1926. Locals call it the 'Wedding Cake', because of its ornate pinnacles and white-stone construction.

Albert Park and Auckland Art Gallery

Opposite the Old Arts Building is **Albert Park** ⓯ (daily 24 hours), a beautifully maintained inner-city sanctum featuring a floral clock, statues of Queen Victoria and influential early colonial leader Sir George Grey (1812–98), a band rotunda and (usually) hordes of students lazing on the grass.

Now take one of the paths that lead downhill to Kitchener Street. On the corner of Wellesley Street is the **Auckland Art Gallery (Toi o Tamaki)** ⓰, heralded in 1888 as 'the first permanent art gallery in the Dominion'. Today, it's the country's largest art institution, with a collection of over 12,500 works, including New Zealand historic, modern and contemporary art, works by Maori and Pacific Island artists, and European paintings, sculpture and prints from 1376 to the present.

It's divided into two galleries: the **Main Gallery** (www.aucklandart gallery.com; daily 10am–5pm; free) displays mainly historical and European art collections, while the **New Gallery** ⓱ (corner of Wellesley and Lorne streets; www.aucklandartgallery. com; daily 10am–5pm; free), which is accessed through a courtyard across the street, showcases cutting-edge contemporary art.

SKY TOWER

To finish, walk one block down Queen Street towards the sea, to Victoria Street, turn left and walk up the slope to Auckland's most prominent landmark, the **Sky Tower** ⓲ (www.skycityauck landtower.co.nz; daily 8.30am–10pm, Fri–Sat until 10.30pm; charge for viewing decks). At 328 metres (1,076ft) high, it's the tallest tower in the southern hemisphere, offering breathtaking views for more than 80km (50 miles) – weather permitting.

If the heart-stopping elevator ride does not provide enough of an adrenaline rush, try the **Sky Jump** (Mission Control, Level 2, SKYCITY; www.sky walkjump.co.nz; daily 10am–5.15pm; charge), a wire-controlled 192-metre

'Sky-jumping' off the Sky Tower

(630ft) leap from a platform near the viewing area.

Adjacent is **SKYCITY** (www.skycity auckland.co.nz; daily 24 hours), home to the Skycity casino, bars and entertainment areas.

Food and drink

❶ MECCA

85–7 Customs Street West, Viaduct Harbour; tel: 09-358 1093; $$

Modern Mediterranean-influenced cuisine, with tasty breakfasts and excellent coffee. Indoor and outdoor seating, and harbour views.

❷ BELLINI

147 Quay Street, Princes Wharf; tel: 09-978 2025; www.bellini.co.nz; $$

This bar at the Hilton Hotel has wonderful harbour views, a comprehensive drinks menu and a good selection of fish and meat dishes.

❸ REVIVE

24 Wyndham Street; tel: 09-303 0420; www.revive.co.nz; $

Tasty and nutritious vegetarian fare, much of which is organic.

❹ CAFÉ MELBA

33 Vulcan Lane; tel: 09-377 0091; www.cafemelba.co.nz; $$

Tucked away on one of the coolest laneways in Auckland, lined with boutique bars and shops, Café Melba serves great coffee, brilliant breakfasts (try the scrambled eggs) and lovely lunches.

❺ VIVACE

50 High Street; tel: 09-302 2303; www.vivacerestaurant.co.nz; $

Italian-style food and a selection of hot and cold tapas, accompanied by an excellent wine list. Lunch and dinner only Monday to Friday; Saturday open from 5pm till late.

❻ WINTERGARDEN CAFÉ

Auckland Domain; tel: 09-354 3360; www.wintergardenpavilion.co.nz; $

With views over duck ponds, gardens and the meandering walkways of the Domain, this is a lovely setting to take tea (and cake). Open for lunch, and morning and afternoon tea.

❼ STRAWBERRY ALARM CLOCK

119 Parnell Road; tel: 09-377 6959; $

This is an unpretentious, laid-back venue, with an enticing range of paninis and brunch dishes. Try the CLAT, a stacked sandwich of chicken, lettuce, avocado and tomato.

❽ VERVE CAFÉ

311 Parnell Road; tel: 09-379 2860; $$

Classic café food at very reasonable prices, the Verve is a relaxing spot with a nice decked area for alfresco dining/drinking.

Dinghy in front of the uninhabited Rangitoto Island

AROUND AUCKLAND

Spend a couple of hours driving around Auckland's waterfront, and then catch a ferry to historic Devonport. If you have time, go further and explore uninhabited Rangitoto Island or verdant Waiheke Island.

DISTANCE: 21km (13 miles), excluding the island tours
TIME: A full day
START/END: Ferry Building, Auckland
POINTS TO NOTE: You will need a car in order to follow this route to the letter. Non-drivers can simply follow the second part of the route and do the island visits. Remember to pack a bathing costume for the beach visits.

Auckland's stunning Waitemata ('sparkling') Harbour and surrounding bays are popular with watersports fans – they also provide the focal point for this tour.

ALONG TAMAKI DRIVE

From the **Ferry Building** ❶ (see page 30), continue east along Quay Street, with the port to your left. Shortly after you pass the container terminal (on your left), Quay Street becomes Tamaki Drive. Hobson Bay is on your left now, and **Parnell Baths** (www.clmnz.co.nz/parnell baths; Nov–Apr Mon–Fri 6am–8pm, Sat–Sun 8am–8pm; charge), an outdoor swimming complex, is on your right. Beyond, across the harbour, the most prominent feature is the volcanic cone of uninhabited **Rangitoto Island**.

Continuing along Tamaki Drive, following the signposts to St Heliers, you will pass **Okahu Bay**, the first of a string of city beaches. On your right is the broad, grassy area of **Orakei Domain**.

KELLY TARLTON'S

As you drive around the bay, watch out on the right for Hammerheads seafood restaurant building; use it as a landmark to move into the righthand lane and turn into the car park at the well signposted **Kelly Tarlton's Sea Life Aquarium** ❷ (23 Tamaki Drive; www.kellytarltons. co.nz; daily 9.30am–5.30pm; charge). There's lots to see and experience here, including an encounter with sharks in the 'Shark Cage'. Acrylic tunnels lead visitors through tanks of exotic local marine life and you can board a 'snow cat' to view penguins – the vehicles plunge through a 'white-out storm' to

Olive trees and vineyard on Waiheke Island

emerge in a re-created Antarctic landscape. Allow two hours here.

MISSION BAY

Resume your journey east for another 1km (0.6 mile) until you arrive at **Mission Bay ❸**. Turn left, off Tamaki Drive into either the first public car park or the second one near the large clock. There are plenty of eating options here, including **Portofino**, see ❶, at the long line of eateries across the road from the beach. Afterwards, stroll along the promenade and go for a paddle.

If you're feeling energetic, tackle the seaside walk east to **Kohimarama ❹**, 2km (1.25 miles) away, or **St Heliers ❺**, a further 1km (0.6 mile), where **Kahve** offers options for satisfying a well-earned appetite – see ❷.

Continue the drive, heading up Cliff Road at the end of Tamaki Drive to **Ladies Bay** and the lookout at **Achilles Point ❻**. Note the plaque honour-

ing HMS *Achilles*, which took part in the 1939 Battle of the River Plate, then retrace your path along Tamaki Drive to the Ferry Building.

ISLAND TOURS

From here, leave the car behind and take a passenger ferry to Devonport, before exploring Rangitoto or Waiheke islands. Note, the last ferry from Devonport to Rangitoto leaves at 12.25pm. (It's also possible to catch a ferry directly from Auckland to Rangitoto, and from Devonport to **Waiheke Island**.)

Devonport and Rangitoto Island

Ferries for the 12-minute crossing to **Devonport ❼** depart half-hourly from the Fullers Cruise Centre (Pier 1, Ferry Building, 99 Quay Street; www.fullers.co.nz; Mon–Thu 6am–11.45pm, Fri–Sat 6am–1.30am, Sun 6.45am–10.45pm; charge). Stroll up Victoria Street from the ferry terminal to the heart of the vil-

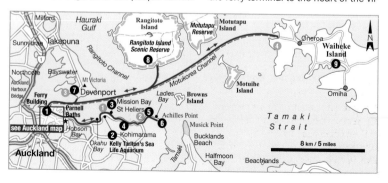

Sunrise over Hauraki Gulf   _Bird's-eye view of Devonport_

lage. For information on sights, pop into the **Devonport i-Site Visitor Centre** (tel: 09-446 0677; daily 8.30am–5pm).

In good weather, consider hiking up the volcanic cones of **Mount Victoria** or **North Head** (check with the information centre for directions) for great views over Auckland, the Waitemata Harbour and the islands of the Hauraki Gulf, or visit Cheltenham Beach to relax and swim. Alternatively, browse Devonport's boutiques and antiques shops and relax at a café such as the **Devonport Stone Oven Bakery and Café**, see ➌.

Catch the ferry from Devonport to **Rangitoto Island** ➑ (the name means 'blood-red sky'). This 600-year-old volcano offers a mix of rugged lava outcrops and caves, lush native bush and sandy coves. Hike to the summit, which, at 260 metres (864ft), delivers more spectacular views of Auckland and the gulf.

Waiheke Island

Another option is to visit **Waiheke Island** ➒ (ferries depart from Auckland's Ferry Building every hour with Fullers, journey time: 40 minutes; ferries leave Devonport for Waiheke every 30 mins Mon–Fri 5.30am–11.45pm, Sat 6am–11.45pm, Sun 7am–10.15pm). Waiheke has beautiful beaches, walking tracks, vineyards, native bush and laid-back seaside villages. Options for exploring include hiring a mountain bike, purchasing a hop-on, hop-off bus pass, or joining a 1.5-hour Explorer Tour or Vineyard Tour through Fullers (www.fullers.co.nz; charge). Alternatively, take it easy at the **Mudbrick Café**, see ➍.

Food and drink

➊ PORTOFINO

71 Tamaki Drive, Mission Bay; tel: 09-528 1212; www.portofino.co.nz; $$
Family owned Italian restaurant, well known for its traditional pizza and pasta dishes.

➋ KAHVE

1 St Heliers Bay Road, St Heliers; tel: 09-575 2919; $
Delicious European fare served in an ambient, renovated 1920s store.

➌ DEVONPORT STONE OVEN BAKERY AND CAFÉ

5 Clarence Street, Devonport; tel: 09-445 3185; $
Bakes 30 varieties of bread, all of which are fat-free and naturally fermented. Sourdough is a speciality. Good range of delicious cakes and pastries, plus excellent espressos.

➍ MUDBRICK CAFÉ

Church Bay Road, Waiheke Island; tel: 09-372 9050; www.mudbrick.co.nz; $$$
The Mudbrick Café offers a winning combination of beautiful vineyard setting, varied menu, indoor and outdoor seating and great views of Auckland across the water.

Fishing in the Bay

NORTHLAND

Kilometres of golden beaches, giant sand dunes, tranquil harbours, bush-clad islands and large tracts of ancient kauri forest are among the highlights on this driving route of the North.

DISTANCE: 977km (607 miles)
TIME: Two to four days
START/END: Auckland
POINTS TO NOTE: You will need a car for this route; for details of car-hire firms, see page 135. Note, however, that hire cars are not insured on Ninety Mile Beach. For details of hotels in this area, see page 107.

Northland, often called the 'birthplace of the nation', is believed to have been the landing point of the Maori adventurer Kupe in the 10th century. It was home to the first seat of government and the *Treaty of Waitangi* was signed here in 1840.

Along Northland's eastern edge is the Bay of Islands, known for its picturesque 800km (500-mile) coastline, which embraces 144 islands. At the northern tip of Northland is Cape Reinga, a place sacred to the Maori. On the West Coast attractions include Hokianga, a sheltered harbour with a score of ragged inlets, and Ninety Mile Beach.

TOWARDS WHANGAREI

Leaving **Auckland** ❶ early via SH1, cross the Auckland Harbour Bridge then continue on SH1, choosing the toll route ($2.20; pay as indicated) following the signs to **Warkworth** ❷. For a breakfast stop, try **The Ginger Café**, see ❶, just under an hour from Auckland.

Waipu and Whangarei

It's 100km (62 miles) from Warkworth to Whangarei. En route you'll pass **Waipu** ❸, a small town with big Scottish links (ever since 900 hardy pioneers emigrated here in the 1700s), where you're greeted with signposts offering *Ceud Mile Failte* ('A hundred thousand welcomes' in Scottish Gaelic). If you're here in early January, you might catch the annual Scottish games, featuring caber-tossing-style action. A good place to stop for a breather and a coffee is **Waipu Cafe and Deli** see ❷.

Whangarei ❹ is Northland's main city and a busy port. As you enter on SH1, look out on the left for Tarewa Park, where there is an information cen-

Ninety Mile Beach   *Wonderful diving off Northland's coast*

tre. If time allows, take a side trip to the **Whangarei Falls**, about 5km (3 miles) north of town, which plunge 25 metres (82ft) into a tranquil, bush-fringed pool. Hike the 20-minute walk around the falls before rejoining SH1.

BAY OF ISLANDS

Kawakawa

Follow the signs to **Kawakawa ❺** (about one hour from Whangarei), gateway to the Bay of Islands. Kawakawa's attractions include the public toilets, which were transformed in 1999 by the Austrian artist Friedensreich Hundertwasser, an Austrian-born artist (1928–2000) who so embraced New Zealand that he apparently kept his watch set on Kiwi time wherever he was. The toilets feature his trademark bright colours, organic forms and prolific use of tiles. For food, try the platform dining at the **Railway Station Café**, see ❸.

Paihia

Leave SH1 and turn off to Opua and **Paihia ❻**, the perfect departure point for exploring the Bay of Islands (Bay of Islands Information Office, Maritime Building, Paihia Wharf; tel: 09-402 7730; www.bayof islandsinformation.co.nz, daily 8am–7pm), named by Captain Cook when he sheltered among them in 1769.

Paihia boasts plenty of good restaurants and hotels and is surrounded by history. New Zealand's first colonists settled in nearby Russell, and modern New Zealand's founding document, the *Treaty of Waitangi*, was signed here in 1840.

A huge range of half-day and day-long cruises and tours are offered by Fullers Bay of Islands (Mari-

Northland beach

time Building, Paihia Wharf; www.dolphin cruises.co.nz).

Russell

Most cruises offer the option of disembarking at **Russell** ❼. Set on a peninsula across the harbour, this is where New Zealand's first white colonialists settled and it was the country's first capital.

Once known as 'the hell hole of the Pacific' and famous for its unruly population of whalers and runaways, it's now a quiet town with a distinctly Victorian atmosphere. Walk along the waterfront to **Pompallier House** (South End, The Strand; www.heritage.org.pompallier.co.nz; daily 10am–5pm; charge), a Catholic mission house dating to 1841, with attractive gardens and fine views of the Bay of Islands.

Also visit the **Russell Museum** (2 York Street; www.russellmuseum.org.nz; daily 10am–4pm; charge), which documents the development of the town from its early days as a Maori village; highlights include a model of Captain Cook's ship the *Endeavour*. Other activities include hiking up Flagstaff Hill.

Take a break from your sightseeing at one of the many fine eateries lining the waterfront. The **Duke of Marlborough**, see ❹, is a good choice for food and for overnight accommodation.

Ferries serve Russell every half-hour (journey time 15 minutes; book at the Maritime Building or pay on board).

Haruru Falls

On your return to Paihia, there are several sights nearby worth visiting, including **Haruru Falls** ❽. To reach the falls drive 3km (2 miles) down Puketona Road, or,

Carved Maori mask

Fun on Te Paki sand dunes

if you're feeling adventurous, explore the waterway by kayak with Coastal Kayakers (Te Karuwha Parade, Ti Bay, Waitangi; www.coastalkayakers.co.nz).

Waitangi Treaty House

Retrace your route and then follow the signs to the **Waitangi National Reserve** ❾ (www.waitangi.orgnet.nz; daily Boxing Day–Feb 9am–6pm, Mar–Christmas Eve 9am–5pm; charge). Allow at least an hour to stroll the grounds and view the **Whare Runanga** (Maori meeting house, which depicts the ancestors of many Maori tribes in its intricate carvings), *waka* (Maori war canoe) and the **Waitangi Treaty House**, where modern New Zealand's founding document was signed in 1840. Have lunch at the Whare Waka Café, located in the Treaty House grounds, or return in the evening for a recommended cultural production performed by local Maori.

TOWARDS CAPE REINGA

At this point you can either do the same route in reverse, going back to Auckland via SH1, return via the West Coast's SH12 or travel north for another 223km (140 miles) to **Cape Reinga**. The round trip to the tip of the North Island can be completed in a day's drive from Paihia but it's worth taking longer. Alternatively, a number of operators run coach and four-wheel-drive tours from Paihia. Most drive one way via Ninety Mile Beach (see page 42) and return by road.

Kerikeri

For those driving north, grab breakfast in the vibrant township of **Kerikeri** ❿ a haven for gourmet travellers, with locally produced wine, olives and avocados, cheese, ice cream and chocolate. For brunch or lunch, try the **Pear Tree,** see ❺.

Mangonui, Awanui and Paparore

Continue north on SH10 through the fishing village of **Mangonui** ⓫, home to New Zealand's best fish-and-chip shop, see ❻. Rejoin SH1 at Awanui. An interesting stop here is **Ancient Kauri Kingdom** (229 SH1, Awanui; www.ancient kauri.co.nz; daily 9am–5pm; free), where 30,000–50,000-year-old swamp kauri logs are crafted into furniture and housewares.

Nearby, in **Paparore** ⓬, the **Gumdiggers Park** (171 Heath Road; www.gum diggerspark.co.nz; daily 9am–5pm; charge) offers an insight into the days when settlers dug for kauri gum (used to make varnish) at its 100-year-old gumfield.

Cape Reinga

Rejoin the northbound SH1 to **Cape Reinga** ⓭. The cape is of great spiritual significance to Maori people, who believe it's 'the place of the leaping', where the souls of the dead gather before they enter the next world. Weather permitting, the **Three Kings Islands**, named by Abel Tasman in 1643, will be visible on the horizon,

Cycling along Ninety Mile Beach

while the spectacular Cape Maria Van Diemen dominates the west.

THE WEST COAST

Ninety Mile Beach
The highlight of a Cape Reinga trip involves driving one way along the magnificent sandy highway of **Ninety Mile Beach**, entering or exiting on **Te Paki Stream** ⑭. Remember, though, hired cars are not insured on the beach (if you're in a hire car, simply head south on SH1.) The vast Te Paki Dunes at the start of the stream can be reached by road, and sand toboggans can be hired locally for sliding down them. Rejoin SH1 or continue south following the beach's unbroken arch of white sand to **Ahipara** ⑮, at the southern tip.

BACK TO AUCKLAND

To return to Paihia, travel via Kaitaia and Kawakawa on SH1. Alternatively, to travel via the West Coast, turn onto SH12 at Ohaeawai. For your first glimpse of Hokianga Harbour, take the turn-off to **Rawene** ⑯, a picturesque harbourside town on a peninsula. Noteworthy buildings here include **Clendon House** (8 Clendon Esplanade; Nov–Apr Sat–Sun 10am–4pm, also open Thu, Fri and Mon in summer school holidays, May–Oct Sun only; charge), an 1860s building that gives an insight into early colonial life.

A good stopping point here is the **Boatshed Café**, see ⑦, where you can watch the vehicular ferry crossing to **Kohukohu**. Jump aboard, if time allows, to explore this once thriving timber town, stamped with early 1900s architecture and featuring NZ's oldest stone bridge.

Opononi
Back on SH12, a 19km (12-mile) drive leads to **Opononi** ⑰, one-time home of Opo, a friendly bottlenose dolphin that adopted the town after being orphaned and played with children throughout the summer of 1955–6, before being mysteriously killed. A bronze statue of the dolphin was unveiled here in 2013.

Omapere and Waipoua Forest
The small town of **Omapere** ⑱ provides a dramatic vista of the Hokianga Harbour before you enter the **Waipoua Forest** on SH12. The forest, home to the massive kauri tree, is an ideal place to wander in the type of dense vegetation that once cloaked New Zealand. There are several walks to enjoy here, the most popular being the five-minute stroll to see the 2,000-year-old Tane Mahuta, the largest kauri of all. For a number of tour options, including twilight experiences, check out Footprints Waipoua (334 State Highway 12, Omapere; www.footprintswaipoua.co.nz; daily; charge).

Kai Iwi Lakes and Baylys Beach
Heading south on SH12, other popular attractions include the Kai Iwi Lakes and the pounding shores of **Baylys Beach** ⑲, before you reach the flats

A massive kauri tree

of **Dargaville** and **Ruawai**, lush with kumara (sweet potato) crops.

Be sure to stop at Matakohe to visit the **Matakohe Kauri Museum** (www. kau.nz; daily 9am–5pm; charge) and lose yourself for a while in bygone days of kauri-felling, gum-digging and hardy pioneers, before rejoining SH1 to Auckland.

Waiwera Thermal Resort

Consider stopping en route at the **Waiwera Infinity Thermal Spa Resort ⑳** (21 Main Road, Waiwera; www.waiwera. co.nz; Mon–Thu 10am–5pm, Fri–Sun 10am–6pm; charge), where you can relax in hot thermal pools before returning to the bustle of the city.

Food and drink

① THE GINGER CAFÉ

21 Queen Street, Warkworth; tel: 09-422 2298; $

A popular bistro-style café serving wholesome fare including an excellent range of wheat-free, dairy-free and gluten-free options.

② WAIPU CAFE & DELI

29 The Centre, Waipu; tel: 09-432 0990; $

Freshly prepared sandwiches, rolls and panini and decent coffee, served by friendly staff. Sunny courtyard garden and dining area.

③ THE RAILWAY STATION CAFÉ

102 Gillies Street, Kawakawa; tel: 09-404 1110; $

Located in Kawakawa's historic railway station with sheltered platform dining, this established café serves simple homemade fare.

④ DUKE OF MARLBOROUGH

35 The Strand, Russell; tel: 09-403 7829; www.theduke.co.nz; $$–$$$

The menu at the restaurant in this smart waterfront boutique hotel has French foundations with strong New Zealand influences. Oysters, mussels and other seafood are brought straight from the sea to the table.

⑤ THE PEAR TREE

215 Kerikeri Road, Kerikeri; tel: 0508-732 78733; www.thepeartree.co.nz; $

Unpretentious food, reasonably priced and served in a stunning riverside setting with great gardens for kids to explore.

⑥ MANGONUI FISH SHOP

Beach Road, Mangonui; tel: 09-406 0478; $

Overhangs the Mangonui Harbour and serves fresh, locally caught fish. Succulent bluenose, served with lemon, is the speciality.

⑦ BOATSHED CAFÉ

8 Clendon Esplanade, Rawene; tel: 09-405 7728; $

Situated in a renovated shed on stilts over the harbour, this café does fresh New Zealand fare. From the terrace watch the mist rising from mangroves as water laps beneath your seat.

Kayaking around Cathedral Cove

COROMANDEL PENINSULA

This two-day driving route leads from the old gold-mining township of Coromandel, across the ranges to Mercury Bay's magnificent Cathedral Cove, then south to the resort area of Pauanui and Tairua.

DISTANCE: 452km (280 miles)
TIME: Two days
START: Auckland
END: Auckland or Tauranga
POINTS TO NOTE: You will need a car for this route. Take care as you approach the Kopu Bridge, which spans the Waihou River. It's a long, one-lane bridge controlled by traffic lights, so make sure you wait until the lights are green. We recommend a mining tour in Thames, for which you'll need sensible footwear with closed toes. Aim to arrive at Hot Water Beach (see page 46) for low tide.

Coromandel Peninsula is one of New Zealand's most ruggedly beautiful regions, with waterfalls, secluded hot springs, huge expanses of windswept beach festooned with driftwood, and old gold mines. In the 19th century, the peninsula was exploited for kauri timber, kauri gum and gold. Areas of forest were axed, but some remain, providing a home for rare species of wildlife, including frogs, kingfishers and cacophonous sea-bird colonies.

Auckland to Thames

Thames, the gateway to the peninsula, is a straightforward 90-minute drive from **Auckland ❶**. From Queen Street, drive up to Karangahape Road; turn left, then veer right before Grafton Bridge, following the signs to SH1. Go south for about 50km (30 miles) and, shortly after Bombay, take the turn-off for SH2, signposted to Tauranga. Follow the highway another 35km (22 miles) before turning east on to SH25, signposted to Thames. The road traverses the low-lying former swamplands of the Hauraki Plains, crosses the Kopu Bridge over the Waihou River. At a T-junction at the base of the Coromandel Range, turn left and drive 5km (3 miles) to Thames.

THAMES

Nowadays, **Thames ❷** is predominantly a service town for outlying rural communities, but in the 19th century its gold-mines sustained the largest population in New Zealand – with 18,000 inhabitants and over 100 hotels.

Behind Thames is the Coromandel Forest Park, with 50km (31 miles) of

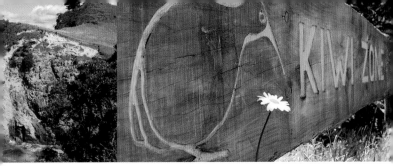

| Coastal cliffs | Kiwi protection area |

well-maintained hiking tracks to explore. The **i-SITE Visitor Centre** (200 Mary Street; tel: 07-868 7284; www.thecoromandel.com/towns/thames; Oct–Mar Mon–Fri 8.30am–5pm, Sat–Sun 9am–4pm; Apr–Sept Mon–Fri 9am–5pm, Sat 9am–1pm, Sun 12–4pm) has more about the region's activities.

Drive Pollen Street, the town's main thoroughfare, for hints about its heyday. Some mining-era buildings remain, notably the restored **Brian Boru Hotel**. The **Sola Café**, see ➊, is open, though, and serves tasty fare.

Mining Town

Follow Pollen Street north and turn right, onto SH25, then quickly right again for the **Goldmine Experience** (corner of SH25 and Moanataiari Road; www.goldmine-experience.co.nz; Jan–Mar daily 10am–4pm, Apr–May and Sept–Dec Sat–Sun 10am–1pm; charge). The original site of the 1868 Gold Crown claim now features a photographic exhibition of Thames. The well-informed hosts will take you on a 40-minute tour of an old mine shaft, which can be muddy. Other activities include gold-panning.

COROMANDEL TOWNSHIP

Continue north on SH25. To your left lies the Firth of Thames, boasting an abundance of birdlife. Some of New Zealand's best driving can be enjoyed here, winding through tiny beachside settlements, interspersed with cliffs gripped by ages-old red-blossoming pohutukawa. If time allows, visit Tararu's exotic **Butterfly and Orchid Garden** (115 Victoria Street, Tararu, Thames; www.butterfly.co.nz; daily 9.30am–4.30pm; charge) and wander through **Rapaura Water Gardens** (586 Tapu-Coroglen Road; www.rapaura.com; daily 9am–5pm; charge).

Walk around **Coromandel ➌**, which has an arty atmosphere, to admire its Victorian buildings and relics from the gold-mining and timber industries. For a feed, head to the **Pepper Tree**, see ➋.

Cathedral Cove

You can try gold-panning and admire the water-wheel at the **Coromandel Stamper Battery** (410 Buffalo Road; tel: 0310-232 8262; tours summer Sat–Thu 10am–3pm; charge). Return to the main road, then turn right for the **Driving Creek Railway and Potteries** (380 Driving Creek Road; www.dcrivingcreekrailway.co.nz; daily 10am–5pm; charge). A narrow-gauge 15in track, with tunnels, spirals and a double-decker viaduct, zig-zags uphill past sculptures to the 'Eyeful Tower', a wooden terminus with gorgeous views of the Firth of Thames. There's also an art gallery, featuring the work of owner and renowned potter Barry Brickell, and wildlife sanctuary.

WHITIANGA

Resume your drive, crossing the Coromandel Range on SH25. En route to Whitianga, visit the beautiful East Coast beaches of Matarangi, Kuaotunu and Opito Bay. **Whitianga ❹** is the main hub for marine-based activities in **Te Whanganui A Hei Marine Reserve**, which stretches from Cooks Bluff and Motukorure Island to Mahurangi Island, with excellent snorkelling opportunities (fishing is prohibited). Pit stops include **Espy Café**, see ❸, opposite the beach, a five-minute walk from the town centre.

HAHEI

In the village of **Hahei ❺**, 16km (10 miles) south, you can rent a kayak for a guided trip to the stunning **Cathedral Cove**, where a gigantic arched cavern penetrates the headland, with **Cathedral Cove Kayaking** (88 Hahei Beach Road; www.seakayaktours.co.nz; daily; charge), or hop aboard the *Hahei Explorer* (6 Wigmore Crescent, Hahei; www.haheiexplorer.co.nz; daily 10am and 2pm; charge). Cathedral Cove can also be reached on foot, via a track that leads down from a lookout point above Hahei.

HOT WATER BEACH

To soak in your own freshly dug pool at **Hot Water Beach ❻**, drive south 10km (6 miles) and turn off, following signs. Aim to arrive around low tide (your accommodation hosts or the visitor centre will know tide times). Bring a spade – or hire one for $5 from **Hot Waves Café**, see ❹ – and stroll north along the beach. A rocky outcrop marks where you can dig holes in the sand. Wallow in the hot-spring waters until the tide begins to turn. Note that it's not safe to swim at Hot Water Beach, owing to strong currents.

TAIRUA AND PAUANUI

Further south on SH25 is the **Tairua ❼** (www.tairua.org.nz), with good beaches for surfing and swimming. The best views of its harbour and white beach can be had from the top of Mount Paku. Maori legend has it that if you climb to the peak of the mountain you'll return

Rural landscape near Hahei

Enjoying the surf on an east–coast beach

within seven years; the outstanding views may entice you to do this anyway.

The neighbouring community of **Pauanui** ❽ is a popular playground for wealthy Aucklanders and a great place to relax. Local activities include swimming, surfing, fishing, diving, bush walks and golf. **Miha Restaurant**, see ❺, is a short stroll from the beach.

BACK TO AUCKLAND

Return to Auckland via SH25A, which travels through the Coromandel Forest Park to Kopu, or continue on to Tauranga (see page 48). Drive 34km (21 miles) south on SH25 to the summer beach resort of **Whangamata**, where beach life reigns, and surfers rule. Fishing is immensely popular, and even swimming with dolphins is not an infrequent occurrence. There are also two good golf courses, mountain biking in the forest and walking trails, including the **Wharekirauponga, Wentworth Valley** and **Luck at Last Mine** tracks. From here it's an easy 100km (62-mile) journey through the gold-mining township of Waihi and on to SH2 to Tauranga.

Food and drink

❶ SOLA CAFÉ
720b Pollen Street, Thames; tel: 07-868 8781; www.solacafe.co.nz; $
In the heart of the Grahamstown area of Thames (to the north of the centre), this vegetarian café serves generous portions, and has a wheat- and gluten-free menu. While you indulge in nutritious fare such as layered eggplant and polenta lasagne, you can check out the work of local artisans decorating the café walls.

❷ PEPPER TREE
31 Kapanga Road, Coromandel Township; tel: 07-866 8211; www. peppertreerestaurant.co.nz; $$
Serves light, fresh Kiwi cuisine at breakfast, lunch and dinner. Try the lamb. Space for indoor and outdoor dining.

❸ ESPY CAFÉ
10 The Esplanade, Whitianga; tel: 07-866 0778; www.espycafewildhogs.co.nz; $–$$
Right on the beach with magnificent views, Espy Café serves delicious coffee and breakfast and lunch dishes with gluten free options. Open from 7.30am until 4pm.

❹ HOT WAVES CAFÉ
8 Pye Place, Hot Water Beach; tel: 07-866 3887; $–$$
Hot Waves serves delicious home-made food in an ambient mud-brick building. Tables spill into a large native bush garden.

❺ MIHA RESTAURANT
42 Mount Avenue, Pauanui Beach; tel: 07-864 8088; $$$
Within Grand Mercure Puka Park Resort, offering Pacific Rim flavours blended with a modern European twist.

Disused wharf pillars in Tauranga Harbour

TAURANGA DISTRICT

This driving route crossing the Tauranga District in the Bay of Plenty can be done from Rotorua, travelling through the kiwifruit-growing area of Te Puke to Mount Maunganui, or in reverse in conjunction with route 4 (see page 44).

DISTANCE: 166km (103 miles)
TIME: A full day
START/END: Rotorua
POINTS TO NOTE: A car is needed for this route. Allow about 90 minutes for the direct return journey from Rotorua to Tauranga. Bring a swimming costume if you want to bathe at the spa at the end of the tour.

The Tauranga District is an easy day trip from Rotorua, 86km (53 miles) along an attractive northbound route. It is part of the Bay of Plenty, an area that the Maori travelled vast distances to reach in a series of migrations over several hundred years. Since then, the relaxed settlements along this coastline have continued to draw visitors from far and wide.

TOWARDS OKERE FALLS

In **Rotorua ❶**, start at the **i-SITE Visitor Centre** on Fenton Street. Turn left and follow SH30 out of town, travelling past Te Ngae and the airport, and continuing straight on SH33 to Okawa Bay and Lake Rotoiti. Make **Okere Falls ❷**, at the head of Lake Rotoiti, your first stop. Take the sharp left turn just past the Okere Falls shop and follow the signs to a small car park. This is the start point of an easy 10-minute walk along the Kaituna River to a lookout point. You can go over its 7-metre (23ft) falls in a whitewater raft with Raftabout (Okere Falls Bridge, SH33; www.raftabout.co.nz; daily 9am, 12.30pm and 3.30pm) – these are the highest commercially rafted waterfalls in the world.

TOWARDS TE PUKE

Continuing for about 25km (15.5 miles) by car from Okere Falls, watch for signs to **Spring Loaded Fun Park ❸** (316 SH33, Paengaroa; www.springloadedfunpark.co.nz; daily 9am–5pm; charge). Here, daredevils can hop aboard a jet-boat up the Kaituna River, learn to four-wheel-drive, or take a scenic helicopter flight.

View from Maunganui   *Kiwifruit Country*

Kiwifruit Country

Shortly after Spring Loaded Fun Park, the road meets SH2. Make a left turn here towards the fertile soils of Te Puke, New Zealand's major kiwifruit-growing area (80 percent of the country's kiwifruit are grown in the Bay of Plenty). Just past the turn-off to Whakatane (from where you can take a boat trip to see an active volcano on White Island) is a sculpture of the giant kiwi fruit that marks **Kiwifruit Country** ❹ (Longridge Park, 316 SH33, Paengaroa; www.kiwifruitcountry.co.nz; daily 9am–5pm, tours 9.30am–4pm; charge); this working kiwifruit farm offers informative rides through the orchards aboard a cart train.

MOUNT MAUNGANUI

A roundabout 16km (10 miles) beyond Te Puke signals the approach of Tauranga and **Mount Maunganui** ❺. Do not veer left on SH2, but continue on what becomes Maunganui Road. Follow it for about 4km (2.5 miles) to reach what locals dub 'The Mount'. This refers to the town's namesake, Maunganui, a conical rocky headland that rises to a height of 232 metres (761ft) and was one of the largest early Maori settlements in New Zealand.

The well-signposted **i-SITE Visitor Centre** (Salisbury Avenue; www.bayofplentynz.com) can provide maps to hiking trails on the mountain. Trace Salisbury Avenue round past the sheltered **Pilot Bay** to the base of The Mount, park near the Domain campgrounds, then follow signs to the start of the tracks. You can either take the Summit Road Track to the top of the mountain, or stroll the circular track around the base. The walkway that leads to the summit is dotted with seats offering amazing harbour, ocean and city views.

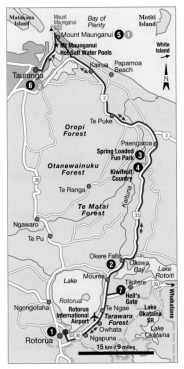

Shady trail leading up Mount Maunganui

Have a picnic on the beach at Pilot Bay or head to Marine Parade to tackle the surf on the sweeping white sands of Mount Maunganui Beach. Inexpensive food can be purchased from any of the cafés that line Maunganui Road, such as **Eighty Eight Café**, see ❶.

TAURANGA

Make your way to **Tauranga ❻**, driving back along Maunganui Road and cutting a sharp right at the roundabout to head along SH29 (Hewletts Road) and over the harbour bridge. As you come off the bridge, follow the signs left at the roundabout to the city centre and park your car on The Strand. Stroll to the north end of **Her-**ries Park** and cross the road to see the ceremonial canoe, *Te Awanui*.

A path at the base of the hill takes you through the pleasant **Robbins Park** and **Rose Garden** to the **Monmouth Military Redoubt**. British troops were stationed here during unrest in the 1860s.

Back on The Strand, a short walk brings you to the main shopping precinct and Devonport Road, where you can enjoy afternoon tea at a local café such as **The Med**, see ❷, before retracing your steps to Rotorua.

Pools and spas

On the way back, stop at the **Mount Maunganui Hot Salt Water Pools** (9 Adams Avenue; www.bayvenuestcal.co.nz; Mon–Sat 6am–10pm, Sun 8am–10pm; charge) for a refreshing swim.

Alternatively, closer to Rotorua, enjoy a communal mud spa overlooking the thermal reserve at **Hell's Gate ❼** (www.hellsgate.co.nz; daily 8.30am–8.30pm; charge), in Tikitere. To get to the pools, turn off SH33 5km (3 miles) after Mourea on to SH30 and travel 4km (2.5 miles), parking right outside the complex. Take a stroll around the thermal park, where highlights include an accessible mud volcano and the beautiful **Kakahi Falls**, the largest hot waterfall in the southern hemisphere, before succumbing to the glorious mud spa. Here you can cake yourself with detoxifying mud, then soak in a hot thermal pool.

Food and drink

❶ EIGHTY EIGHT CAFÉ

88 Maunganui Road; tel: 07-574 0384; $

No nonsense café serving good, honest food and fantastic coffee to loyal locals and happy visitors.

❷ THE MED

62 Devonport Road, Tauranga; tel: 07-577 0487; www.medcafe.co.nz; $

Tasty all-day breakfasts, deli-style salads, pastries and sandwiches, and a range of hot dishes on a blackboard menu.

Having a crazy time Zorbing

ROTORUA

Set amid crater lakes, Rotorua offers stunning scenery in an active volcanic wonderland of spouting geysers, bubbling mud pools, fumaroles and natural thermal springs. This driving route covers its highlights.

> **DISTANCE:** 33km (20 miles)
> **TIME:** At least a full day
> **START/END:** Rotorua
> **POINTS TO NOTE:** A car is needed for this route. Bring a swimming costume if you want to bathe at the Polynesian Spa.

Rotorua, locals proudly boast, is the only place in New Zealand where you can tell exactly where you are with your eyes closed. They're referring, of course, to the distinctive aroma of sulphur that permeates the town, courtesy of its boiling mud pools and hot springs. To visit Rotorua with your eyes shut would be a travesty, however, because it's an area of rich cultural and scenic beauty. Block your nose and head out boldly – you'll soon become accustomed to the smell.

The town was a tourist destination in the 1800s, when visitors came to marvel at the naturally formed Pink and White Terraces (see page 54). Today, it's still one of the country's jewels, a place of thermal wonders, lush forests, green pastures and crystal-clear lakes abounding with fighting trout.

This is the place to dive out of your comfort zone into thrill-seeking activities, from Zorbing to simulated flight. But Rotorua is also a major centre for Maori culture – one third of the city's population is Maori. *Marae* (tribal meeting-places) dot the area.

GONDOLA RIDE

Starting from the Rotorua **i-SITE Visitor Centre** (1167 Fenton Street; www.rotoruanz.com; daily 7.30am–6pm), turn left onto Arawa Street, then right onto Ranolf Street (the start of SH5). This drive takes you past **Kuirau Park** on your left, a 25-hectare (62-acre) public reserve (free) where you can pull over to see several steaming fumeroles.

Continue on, following Ranolf Street as it morphs into Lake Road. At the traffic lights at the end of Lake Road, turn right onto Fairy Springs Road. Travel about 4.5km (3 miles), then turn left into the car park at **Skyline Skyrides Gondola** ❶ (www.skylineskyrides.co.nz; daily 9am–late; charge). Within minutes of buying

Cycling is a great way to tour Rotorua

a ticket you will be whisked sharply up the 900-metre (2,953ft) slopes of Mount Ngongotaha for glorious views of the region that you will soon be exploring; there's also a **café** here, see ❶.

On the return journey, ride back down on the gondola or take the luge, a three-wheel cart, on the exciting 1km (0.6-mile) -long downhill track.

Rainbow Springs

A further 100 metres along Fairy Springs Road is **Rainbow Springs Kiwi Wildlife Park** ❷ (www.rainbow springs.co.nz; daily Oct–Mar 8.30am–10.30pm, Apr–Sept 8.30am–10pm; charge), showcasing more than 150 species of native New Zealand fauna set among freshwater springs and pools filled with rainbow and brown trout. A highlight is the Kiwi Experience, a behind-the-scenes glimpse at a kiwi nursery.

AROUND LAKE ROTORUA

Follow SH5 back towards town, turning off onto Lake Road. Stop at the lakefront parking area near the jetty, where the *Lakeland Queen* (www.lakelandqueen.

com; charge), a 22-metre (72ft) paddle steamer, takes passengers around **Lake Rotorua** from the **Lakeland Queen Launch Jetty** ❸ on foodie cruises.

While aboard you'll be regaled with the love story of Hinemoa and Tutanekai,

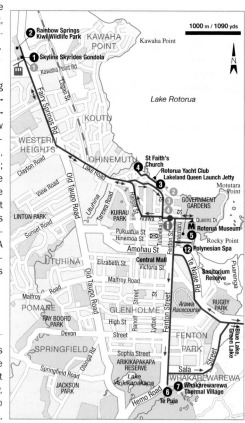

Rotorua thermal pools   _Rafting Kaituna Falls_

a Maori legend similar to _Romeo and Juliet_, but with a happier ending. (If you miss the boat, you can eat at the **Lakeside Café**, see ②.)

Ohinemutu

After lunch take a stroll northwest of the café along the narrow driveway that heads past the **Rotorua Yacht Club** and along the waterfront to **St Faith's Church** and **Ohinemutu** ④. This tiny lakefront village was the main settlement here when Europeans arrived in the 1800s. Today it's renowned for its idyllic little church, built in 1885, with its beautiful stained-glass window depicting a Maori Christ figure who looks as though he is walking on the waters of Lake Rotorua. The church was presented to the Maori people of Rotorua in appreciation of their loyalty to the Crown. Ohinemutu also has raised graves, laid out in this way because of the thermal activity below ground.

Leaving the lakefront, walk to the north end of **Tutanekai Street**, Rotorua's café hotspot; dining options include **The Thai Restaurant**, see ③, **The Indian Star**, see ④, and **Solace Café & Restaurant**. Further south you'll find a wide variety of shops.

Museum of Art and History

Now head east on Arawa Street and Queens Drive, past the Convention Centre and into the Government Gardens. Within its grounds is the **Rotorua Museum** ⑤ (Queen's Drive; www.rotoruamuseum. co.nz), a 1908 Tudor-style building which showcases art exhibitions and whose exhibits tell the story of the local Te Arawa people and the devastating eruption of Mount Tarawera in 1886. The museum is currently closed for earthquake strengthening, but it is still possible to visit the grounds (tours daily 11am and 2pm; free).

WHAKAREWAREWA

Whakarewarewa (pronounced far-car-rear-wah-rear-wah) is the closest thermal area to the city. To reach its two major attractions, head to the **Rotorua i-SITE Visitor Centre** (1167 Fenton Street) and travel south for 3km (2 miles), following the road as it veers right into Hemo Road. On the left is **Te Puia** ⑥ (Hemo Road; www. tepuia.com; daily Sept–Apr 9am–6pm, Apr–Sept 8am–5pm; charge), home of the famous Pohutu Geyser and the New Zealand Maori Arts and Crafts Institute, where you can watch Maori carvers and flax weavers at work. Guided tours leave on the hour, every hour until 5pm and take in the works of the arts institute as well as bubbling mud pools, boiling hot springs, and the Pohutu Geyser, which erupts up to 30 metres (98ft) high.

Allow at least 2–3 hours to explore this area and the adjacent **Whakarewarewa Thermal Village** ⑦ (17 Tryon Street; www.whakarewarewa.com; daily 8.30am–5pm; charge). You can take a guided tour and meet the Tuhourangi/Ngati Wahiao people who live among the geothermal activity and make use of the energy garnered from hot springs and

Mud, glorious mud

steam vents for cooking purposes, as well as the natural mineral waters for communal bathing. The area's geysers can be viewed from safe platforms.

BLUE AND GREEN LAKES

From Whakarewarewa, it's a scenic 20-minute drive to the Blue and Green Lakes. Head back up Fenton Street towards town and turn right into Sala Street; follow the street out to Te Ngae Road (SH30) and then turn off on Tarawera Road, the first main road to your right. Approximately 10km (6 miles) from the city, along the forest-fringed Tarawera Road, you suddenly drop down to opalescent **Lake Tikitapu**, otherwise known as the **Blue Lake** ❽.

Weather permitting, this is a great place for a swim; alternatively, you can hike around its shoreline (1.5 hours) or hire a canoe or pedal boat from the Blue Lake Holiday Park (www.bluelaketop10. co.nz) across the road.

Continuing on, the road rises to a crest, from which you can see Lake Tikitapu and the larger **Lake Rotokakahi**, or **Green Lake** ❾, resting side by side. The waters of the Green Lake are *tapu* (sacred) to local

Maori, and are not open for watersports.

PINK AND WHITE TERRACES

The road continues along a historic tourist route to the former **Pink and White Terraces**, once described as the eighth wonder of the world. The naturally formed silica terraces on the shores of Lake Rotomahana were like a giant staircase, with a fan-shaped edge spilling across almost 300 metres of lakefront. But nature proved unkind to its own wonders, and on 10 June 1886 a massive volcanic eruption of Mount Tarawera obliterated the terraces and buried two Maori villages beneath layers of ash and mud.

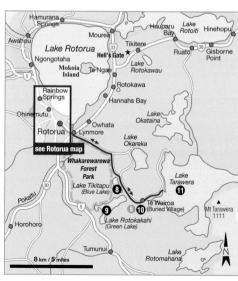

Spectacular views of the Tarawera Crater

A memorial to the tragedy is located a short drive past the Green Lake – the **Buried Village** ❿ excavation of Te Wairoa (1180 Tarawera Road; www.buriedvillage. co.nz; daily Oct–Feb 9am–5pm, Mar–Sept 9am–4.30pm; charge). Parking is available in front of the Buried Village souvenir shop and **Vi's Teahouse**, see ❺.

LAKE TARAWERA

From the Buried Village, Tarawera Road continues to **Lake Tarawera** ⓫. A lookout point en route provides good views of Mount Tarawera across the lake. Take the first left downhill to **Tarawera Landing**, located on a quiet pumice-fringed bay with a small jetty. Lake cruises, guided trout fishing charters, and self-drive boats, kayaks and pedal boats can be hired from The Landing Café.

End your Rotorua day with a soak in thermally heated water. Retrace the route back to Fenton Street and turn right into Hinemoa Street to the lakeside **Polynesian Spa** ⓬ (Lake End, Hinemoa Street; www.polynesianspa.co.nz; daily 8am–11pm; charge). Enjoy a relaxing dip in restorative geothermal waters and treat yourself to a therapeutic massage.

Food and drink

❶ MARKET KITCHEN CAFÉ

Fairy Springs Road; tel: 07-347 0027; $
Menu ranges from all-day breakfast to sandwiches and cakes, fish and chips to pizzas and sushi. Priced as you'd expect at the top of a gondola.

❷ LAKESIDE CAFÉ

Memorial Drive; tel: 07-349 2626; $–$$
If you miss the boat, or choose not to sail, 50 metres/yds to your left (facing the lake) is the Lakeside Café and Crafts Shop, where you can have lunch and browse through a selection of works by local artisans.

❸ THE THAI RESTAURANT

1141 Tutanekai Street; tel: 07-348 6677; www.thethairestaurant.co.nz; $

Authentic country style Thai cuisine with robust flavours. A lively night market is held nearby on Thursday evenings.

❹ THE INDIAN STAR

1118 Tutanekai Street; tel: 07-343 6222; www.indianstar.co.nz;
$–$$
Fully licensed or BYO wine. The Indian Star offers a wide-ranging feast of Indian cuisine. This is where locals come to order their takeouts.

❺ VI'S TEAHOUSE

Tarawera Road; tel: 07-362 8287; $
The café within the Buried Village offers home-cooked fare such as cakes, biscuits, slices, freshly filled rolls and hot savouries, but Devonshire cream tea has been the speciality since it opened in 1910.

Morning on Lake Taupo

TAUPO

This driving route is an easy day trip from Rotorua, heading south to Orakei Korako, then on to Huka Falls and Lake Taupo, New Zealand's largest lake. Stay another day and drive the volcanic loop around the mountainous Tongariro National Park.

DISTANCE: 96km (59 miles), excluding Tongariro National Park; 343km (213 miles) including the park
TIME: One to two days
START: Rotorua
END: Rotorua or Wellington
POINTS TO NOTE: You will need a car for this route. Book in advance for any therapeutic treatments you might want at Taupo Hot Springs (see page 59).

Lake Taupo is fed by sparkling ice-melt from the mountains of the Tongariro National Park. It was formed by volcanic activity – an eruption so large it was recorded by Chinese and Roman writers – and is the focal point of a region full of extraordinary landscapes, unique cultural experiences and incredible adventure opportunities.

The township of Taupo is situated on the shores of the lake, about 90km (56 miles) south of Rotorua. From the **i-SITE Visitor Centre** (1167 Fenton Street) at **Rotorua ❶**, follow the road south past **Whakarewarewa** onto SH5.

THERMAL WONDERLAND

For a day tour, choose one option from the three thermal parks listed below. If you overnight in Taupo, you'll fit in at least two.

Waimangu Volcanic Valley

About 20km (12.5 miles) south of Rotorua on SH5 you'll pass the turn-off to **Waimangu Volcanic Valley ❷** (587 Waimangu Road; www.waimangu.com; daily 8.30am–5pm; charge), a hotbed of thermal activity unearthed by the 1886 eruption of Mount Tarawera. Attractions here include the volcanic area around Waimangu Cauldron, the Inferno Crater, Ruamoko's Throat, various craters, volcanic lakes and hot springs, and a boat cruise to see the steaming cliffs of Lake Rotomahana. A walk through the valley, returning by shuttle bus (excluding the boat ride), takes about one to two hours.

Wai-o-Tapu

About 10km (6 miles) south you'll pass the turn-off for the **Wai-o-Tapu Ther-**

Huka Falls

mal Wonderland ❸ (Loop Road; www.waiotapu.co.nz; daily 8.30am–5pm; charge), famous for the boiling Champagne Pool that flows over green silicate terraces, and the **Lady Knox Geyser**, which, with a little human assistance (eco-friendly soap is used to release the surface tension) blows its top at 10.15am each day. Allow at least an hour.

Lake Ohakuri

Just past Golden Springs, look for signposts to **Orakei Korako** ❹ (494 Orakei Korako Road; www.orakeikorako.co.nz; daily 8am–4.30pm; charge) on the shores of **Lake Ohakuri**, where boats ferry travellers to a pristine geothermal field surrounded by unique silica terraces. Encompassing 35 active geysers, plopping mud pools and fizzing hot springs, this park also features an extremely rare geothermal cave. Dedicate an hour to explore, minimum.

WAIRAKEI PARK

Rejoin SH5 and keep going south. Shortly before **Wairakei** ❺, SH5 joins SH1. Just past Wairakei, on your left, look for the turn-off to the **Volcanic Activity Centre** which is temporarily closed for relocation to Turangi; www.volcanoes.co.nz; Mon–Fri 9am–5pm, Sat–Sun 10am–4pm; charge). The centre has informative displays on the region's geography.

This section of the Waikato River boasts the world's only geothermal prawn farm, the **Huka Prawn Park** (Wairakei Park, Taupo; www.hukaprawnpark.co.nz; daily 9.30am–3.30pm; charge), where you can feast on juicy tropical prawns while enjoying

Tongariro served as Mordor in the Lord of the Rings movies

views of the river as it begins its 425km (264-mile) journey to the sea.

Also in the park is the **Honey Hive** (Wairakei Park; www.hukahoneyhive taupo.com; daily 9am–5pm; free), the country's largest honey centre, selling honey-scented soaps, lotions and wine. There's also honey-tasting, a picnic area and a ride for children.

Follow signs for a thrilling spin on the Waikato River with Huka Jet boat rides (Wairakei Park; www.hukafallsjet.com; daily 10am–4.30pm, departures every half-hour), which take you (at white-knuckle pace) right to the bottom of dramatic Huka Falls.

HUKA FALLS

The most stunning feature in this area is the thundering **Huka Falls** ❻. To reach them, turn left and follow signs 2km (1.25 miles) to the Huka Falls car park. A short walk delivers views of the falls, where up to 270 cubic metres (9,535 cubic ft) of water are tumultuously pushed through a long, narrow gorge before plunging into a deep pool. There are several good walks here.

Pit stops on the Huka Falls Road include **Café Pinot**, see ❶.

TAUPO

From here it's a short drive to **Taupo** ❼. Pause at the signposted lookout on the left heading into town, for panoramic views of the lake and the mountains of Tongariro National Park. It seems serene, but don't be fooled – over the past 27,000 years this crater has erupted 28 times, most recently 1,800 years ago. Hot springs and spas prove this region has not yet run out of steam. Proof of the region's volatile geology can be seen at the Tangiwai rail disaster memorial, on SH49 between Ohakune and Waiouru. Here, in 1953, a lahar flooded the Whangaehu River, destroying the Tangiwai Railway Bridge and killing 153 people. Fortunately, when Mount Ruapehu's Crater Lake burst its banks again, in 2007, an alarm system provided a warning.

Follow SH1 into Taupo township. The Taupo **i-SITE Visitor Centre** (Tongariro Street, Taupo; www.greatlaketauponz.com; daily 8.30am–5pm) is on your right as you enter the town.

Lake Taupo

Lake Taupo regularly plays host to international watersports events and is popular with residents and visitors alike for sailing, kayaking, windsurfing and numerous other sports and activities. Follow the road to the wharf and marina, where various cruises depart across **Lake Taupo** throughout the day. Highly recommended is a trip on the *Ernest Kemp*, a replica 1920s steamer, which leaves daily at 10.30am and 2pm, with an extra sailing at 5pm during summer (www.ernestkemp.co.nz; charge).

Alternatively, hop aboard a catamaran with Chris Jolly Outdoors (14 Rauhoto Street, Taupo Boat Harbour; www.

The mountains in winter

chrisjolly.co.nz; daily 10.30am,1.30pm, 2pm and 5pm; charge) and cruise around Acacia Bay and Rangatira Point, bound for Whakaipo Bay, where contemporary Maori rock carvings can be seen on a cliff face.

For refreshment, walk north up Tongariro Street and take the third right, Horomatangi Street; **Salute Deli Café**, see ❷, is at number 47.

Bungy-jumping and hot springs

Hold lunch if you're planning to bungy-jump over the **Waikato River** with **Taupo Bungy** (202 Spa Road, Taupo; www.taupobungy.co.nz; daily 8.30am–5pm; charge). Also located on site is Taupo's newest attraction, the **Taupo Cliffhanger**, an extreme swing that sees participants reach speeds of up to 70kmh (44mph). From the lower car park it's an easy walk to the river's edge, where you can paddle in a natural hot spring that mixes with cold river water.

Alternatively, soak in thermal pools ranging from 37°C to 41°C (99–106°F), at **Taupo DeBretts** (76 Napier–Taupo Highway; www.taupodebretts.co.nz; daily 7.30am–9.30pm; charge), followed by a therapeutic massage. Booking is essential.

Day-trippers should retrace their steps to Rotorua. To continue the route, stay overnight in Taupo (see page 108).

VOLCANIC LOOP

The first stop on the second day is Tongariro National Park, which offers blue and emerald lakes, waterfalls, rocky plateaux, twisted thickets of native bush, huge open landscapes and snowy slopes, and can easily be explored from Taupo or en route to Wellington.

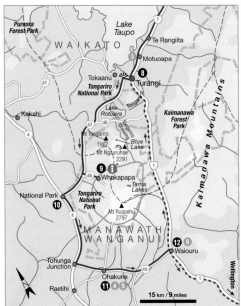

Skiing at Whakapapa

Turangi

Head out of Taupo on SH1, drive through Motuoapa – where **Licorice Café**, see ❸, makes a good breakfast stop – to **Turangi** ❽, a village on the banks of the Tongariro River. Turangi is the place to rediscover the thrill of angling (remember, much river fishing in New Zealand operates on a catch-and-release basis) or to go whitewater rafting with **Tongariro River Rafting** (www.trr.co.nz; departures daily: summer 9am and 2pm, winter noon; charge).

Tongariro National Park

Leaving Turangi on SH47, stop at the lookout on the right before continuing the ascent through dense forest into **Tongariro National Park**. Beneath

---

Tongariro Crossing

The 17km (10.5-mile) Tongariro Crossing, said to be New Zealand's best one-day hike, passes the steep, charred sides of Ngauruhoe, the mineral-stained walls and active fumeroles of Tongariro's Red Crater, and the vivid Emerald Lakes, contrasting sharply with the burnt earth hues of the surrounding lunar-like landscape. Further on is the gleaming Blue Lake, also known as Te Rangihiroa's Mirror, after the son of a chief who explored the region in AD 1750. The views are spectacular. The hike finishes on SH46, and transport to and from the track can be organised at all local hotels.

Mount Tongariro, with its red craters, is **Lake Rotoaira** and the **Opotaka Historic Reserve** (free).

After passing the reserve, you'll see brown, windswept plains of toitoi, manuka and flax, then the charred cinder cone of **Mount Ngauruhoe**, which last erupted in 1975. Mangatepopo Road provides access to the Tongariro Crossing, popularly considered to be New Zealand's best one-day hike.

The majestic snowy crown of **Mount Ruapehu** dominates the route (SH48) to **Whakapapa** ❾, a small ski village with a range of accommodation and cafés. The Visitor Centre provides information on local hikes, including the Mount Ruapehu summit walk (unmarked), Taranaki Falls and Tama Lakes.

If your budget allows, take a scenic flight with **Mountain Air** (corner of SH47 and SH48; www.mountainair.co.nz; daily 8am–5pm). Alternatively, continue on SH47 to the township of **National Park** ❿, a mecca for snow junkies in the ski season, with a climbing wall, equipment hire and bars and cafés.

Ohakune

Follow SH4 south to Tohunga Junction, then turn off onto SH49 to **Ohakune** ⓫, a fast-growing après ski hub. Ohakune offers easy access to the Turoa ski slopes up the picturesque mountain road, dense with mountain beech forest, dwarf shrubs, and alpine flowers. Quality lunch spots here include the **Mountain Kebabs** and **Utopia Café**, see ❹ and ❺.

Natural steam bath

Mountain fun

Waiouru

From Ohakune, SH49 continues on to rejoin SH1 at **Waiouru** ⓬, home to New Zealand's Army's largest training camp and the **Army Memorial Museum** (SH1, Waiouru; www.armymuseum.co.nz; daily 9am–4.30pm; charge), where a sensitively curated collection of army memorabilia captivates military enthusiasts and civilians alike. The museum café, **Home Fires**, see ⓺, is a good place for a break.

From here, you can return to Taupo via SH1, travelling through the dry, desolate landscape of the Rangipo 'desert', before retracing your route back to Rotorua; alternatively, continue south towards Wellington. The 370km (236-mile) journey on SH1 takes around five hours from Taupo. It's 261km (162 miles) and four hours from Waiouru, travelling through Taihape, Bulls, Levin, and down the Kapiti Coast to Wellington.

Food and drink

⓵ CAFÉ PINOT

56 Huka Falls Road, Taupo; 07-376 0260: www.hukafallsresort.com;
$$
Tuck into fine wine and classy cuisine in an exquisite setting, overlooking landscaped gardens and pinot noir vines. Excellent for lunch and dinner.

⓶ SALUTE DELI CAFÉ

47 Horomatangi Street, Taupo; tel: 07-377 4478; $
If you are after a super-fresh salad or grilled sandwich, this is the place to visit.

⓷ LICORICE CAFÉ

57 SH1, Motuoapa, Turangi; tel: 07-386 5551; $
Licorice Café is where those in the know go. The menu changes daily but always features a total of six gluten-free and vegetarian meals, plus a range of other

home-cooked Kiwi fare, including the ever-popular wood-smoked salmon salad.

⓸ MOUNTAIN KEBABS

29 Clyde Street, Ohakune; tel: 0800 532 227; $
The name says it all – freshly made, reasonably priced kebabs are found here. On a mountain.

⓹ UTOPIA CAFÉ

47 Clyde Street, Ohakune; tel: 06-385 9120; $–$$
Great coffee, all-day breakfasts and delicious café fare served throughout the day until 4–5pm. Open fire in winter.

⓺ HOME FIRES CAFÉ

SH1, Waiouru; tel: 06-387 6911; $
This popular café, housed in Waiouru's Army Memorial Museum, serves breakfast from early in the morning, and hearty gourmet burgers, stuffed with the likes of chicken, brie and cranberry, for lunch.

Bird's-eye view of Wellington harbour

WELLINGTON

Vibrant Wellington, the seat of government and the unofficial cultural centre of the country, has a cosmopolitan buzz. This full-day walking route explores its many highlights.

DISTANCE: 4km (2.5 miles)
TIME: A full day
START: Museum of New Zealand
END: Courtenay Place
POINTS TO NOTE: Enjoy a leisurely start to this tour, as the Museum of New Zealand only opens at 10am.

Wellington has an assurance and an international flair that comes with being the country's artistic and cultural heart, as well as its capital city. There's history too – evidence of early Maori settlement can be found at sites all across the Peninsula. With a regional population of about 440,000, including about 200,000 in the city itself, Wellington is, however, considerably smaller than its northern rival, Auckland, which it replaced as capital in 1865.

Although a quiet, unassuming place until the late 20th century, in recent decades New Zealand's capital has blossomed into a dynamic, urban destination with a lively nightlife. The city's charm derives partly from its quirky topography, with wooden turn-of-the-20th-century houses clinging to steep hillsides bristling with native bush and clumps of arum lilies. Zigzag streets spill downwards to the heart of the city, the harbour and the affluent promenade of Oriental Bay. The layout reminds some visitors of San Francisco.

Wellington is nicknamed the 'Windy City', and for good reason; it's usually breezy, and sometimes the wind can knock you over. In the business district, old higgledy-piggledy Wellington has virtually been replaced by soaring modern buildings – a cause of regret for many who loved the haphazard character of the old layout.

MUSEUM OF NEW ZEALAND

The route starts at the **Museum of New Zealand – Te Papa Tongarewa** ❶ (55 Cable Street; www.tepapa.govt. nz; daily 10am–6pm; free), which has a vast collection incorporating interactive displays, virtual-reality games and special exhibitions – some permanent, others visiting.

Art at the Museum of New Zealand

Don't miss the permanent exhibition of Maori myths and legends of creation. The earliest name for Wellington, from Maori legend, is Te Upoko o te Ika a Maui, meaning 'the head of Maui's fish'; caught and pulled to the surface by Polynesian navigator Maui, the fish became the North Island. Also check out the simulated earthquake, displays of bones of the extinct giant moa (a huge flightless bird) and the swingbridge walk through a section of re-created native bush.

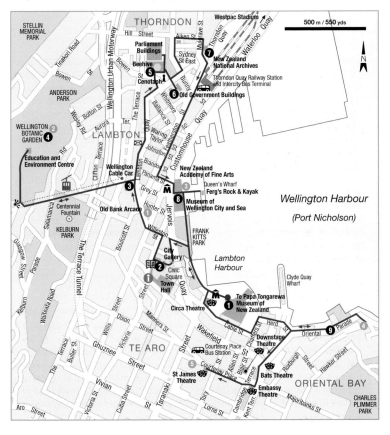

Outside the Museum of New Zealand

CITY CENTRE

Head north, following the waterline towards the city's commercial centre. Watch for in-line skaters as you make your way past the rowing clubs by **Frank Kitts Park**. Situated across the road is the city's vast **Civic Square** ❷, home to the **Michael Fowler Centre** (a concert and conference hall), the Edwardian-style **Town Hall** and the **Wellington City Library**, a gorgeous plaster curve of a building, decorated with metal palms. Tucked away between these civic buildings is the Art Deco **City Gallery** (www.citygallery.org.nz; daily 10am–5pm; free), known for its contemporary art exhibitions – here you'll find the Nikau Café and the Wellington **i-SITE Visitor Centre** (www.wellingtonnz.com; daily 8.30am–5pm).

Lambton Quay

Leave the square via the archway next to the library, cross Victoria Street and walk one block north to Willeston Street. Turn left. Willeston merges with **Lambton Quay**, the heart of the city's commercial and retail area. There was once a quay here, before an earthquake in 1855 pushed a rocky ledge around the harbour's edge, after which the land was reclaimed for the expanding city.

Stroll and window-shop through the stunning Victorian **Old Bank Arcade**, on the corner of Hunter Street and Lambton Quay. Wellington's shopping scene is superb, and it's paired with a fabulous café culture – sample some sublime coffee at **The Astoria**, see ❶. Discover more about Wellington's vibrant culinary scene on a **Zest Food Tour** (www.zestfoodtours.co.nz), during which guides reveal their favourite gourmet hot spots.

Wellington Cable Car

About 150 metres up Lambton Quay you'll see the sign for the **Wellington Cable Car** ❸ (Lambton Quay; www.wellingtoncablecar.co.nz; Mon–Fri 7am–10pm, Sat 8.30am–10pm, Sun 8.30am–9pm; charge). Cars leave every 10 minutes and take you effortlessly up a steep incline, under the motorway and over Kelburn Park to Upland Road for splendid views. There's an excellent viewing point at the upper terminus.

Adjacent to this is the **Wellington Cable Car Museum** (1 Upland Road; www.cablecarmuseumswellington.org.co.nz; daily 9.30am–5pm; free).

BOTANIC GARDEN

Wend through **Wellington Botanic Garden** ❹ (daily dawn–dusk; free): 25 hectares (62 acres) of protected native forest, conifers, specialised plant collections and floral displays, classified as a Garden of National Significance by the Royal New Zealand Institute of Horticulture and a Historic Places Trust Heritage Area.

Wellington Cable Car

The Beehive, seat of power

Wander off the main paths to appreciate the gardens fully, but aim for the **Education and Environment Centre** (Mon–Fri 9am–4pm, Sat–Sun 10am–4pm), where you can learn about New Zealand's flora.

Grab some lunch in the **Picnic Cafe**, see ②, before returning to the cable car.

THE BEEHIVE

Turn left onto Lambton Quay and walk to the end where it meets Bowen Street. Cross over and you are at the circular **Beehive** ⑤, the seat of political power in New Zealand. Designed by British architect Sir Basil Spence and constructed 1969–80, it houses the executive wing of Parliament, including the office of the Prime Minister. Walk past the **Cenotaph**, through the gates, and follow the sweeping drive up to the Beehive and the adjacent **Parliament Buildings**, dating to 1922.

Head to the Visitor Centre (Mon–Fri 10am–4pm, Sat 10am–3pm, Sun 11am–3pm; free) in the foyer for an informative 1-hour guided tour that runs on the hour and reveals how the building was 'earthquake-proofed' during its last renovation.

Old Government Buildings

Also of interest here are the **Old Government Buildings** ⑥, set opposite the Cenotaph on Lambton Quay. Claimed to be the largest wooden building in the southern hemisphere, this was erected in 1876 using over 9,290 sq metres (100,000 sq ft) of timber.

National Archives

Walk down Aiken Street to Mulgrave Street. At the **National Archives** ⑦ (10 Mulgrave Street; www.archives.govt.nz; Mon–Fri 9am–5pm; free), you can view New Zealand's national records, including the modern nation's founding document, the *Treaty of Waitangi*.

QUEEN'S WHARF AREA

Wander back into town along Mulgrave Street, past Thorndon Quay Railway Station, then continue straight along Featherston Street for several blocks to the intersection with Panama Street. Turn left onto Panama and cross **Customhouse Quay** to Queen's Wharf. Here, the **New Zealand Academy of Fine Arts** (www.nzafa.com; daily 10am–5pm; free) exhibits a range of arts and crafts.

Nearby, housed in the 1892 Bond Store Building, is the **Museum of Wellington City and Sea** ⑧ (www.museumsofwellington.orgco.nz; daily 10am–5pm; free), which has a captivating collection of maritime memorabilia, covering the city's seafaring history from early Maori interaction to the 1900s. Highlights include a 12-minute show retelling Maori creation stories. Afterwards, pop into **Bin44** for a drink, see ③.

St James Theatre

ORIENTAL PARADE

If time permits, walk back to the Museum of New Zealand – Te Papa Tongarewa on Cable Street. Carry on around the waterfront, following Cable Street to **Oriental Parade** ❾, where a stroll around the boardwalk gives great views over the harbour and bays – note Wellington's prime residential real estate, clinging to the slopes of Mount Victoria. Call in at the **Boat Café**, see ❹.

COURTENAY PLACE

Return via Courtenay Place, Wellington's main entertainment precinct. At the intersection with Kent Terrace is the grand old **Embassy Theatre**, venue of the world premiere of the final cinematic instalment of *The Lord of the Rings* trilogy.

Further up Courtenay Place, on the left, is the **St James Theatre** (77–87 Courtenay Place; www.venueswellington. com), which hosts musical acts and is home to **Mojo Café**, see ❺.

Food and drink

❶ THE ASTORIA
159 Lambton Quay; tel: 04-473 8500; www.astoria.co.nz; $$
Reminiscent of a Viennese coffee house, this busy café is a favourite haunt of the corporate crowd. Come here for snacks, light lunches and dinner and, of course, the coffee.

❷ PICNIC CAFÉ
The Begonia House, Lady Norwood Rose Garden; tel: 04-472 6002; www.picniccafe. co.nz; $
You'll have to stroll through the gardens to find this gem, but it's worth the walk when you tuck into the tasty, fresh fare while looking over the rose gardens.

❸ BIN44
3 Queens Wharf; tel: 04-499 4450; www.bin44.co.nz; $–$$

Put a bit of class in your glass at this café, restaurant and bar, which does a selection of fine wines, craft beers and speciality coffees as well as meals throughout the day.

❹ BOAT CAFÉ
Oriental Parade; tel: 04-939 3935; www.boatcafe.co.nz; $$
Quality café and restaurant located on a boat bobbing on the harbour. Enjoy brunch or dinner in amazing surrounds, often with live music to follow. The menu offers burgers, salads and seafood chowder in the day and more sophisticated fare in the evening.

❺ MOJO CAFÉ
Westpac St James Theatre, Courtenay Place; tel: 04-801 4231; $
Located just inside the entrance to the theatre, this is the perfect place to conclude the day's sightseeing and plan your evening's entertainment over a coffee.

Martinborough Wine Centre

THE WAIRARAPA

This route takes you out of Wellington, over the Rimutaka Ranges and into the Wairarapa region. Highlights include Martinborough's vineyards, Greytown's colonial architecture and the imposing, rugged coastline.

DISTANCE: 202km (125 miles) return, or 346km (214 miles) including South Coast
TIME: At least one day
START/END: Wellington
POINTS TO NOTE: You will need a car for this route. Martinborough is an 81km (50-mile) drive from Wellington, but the tour takes longer than expected because the road over the Rimutaka Ranges is so winding. To avoid rush-hour congestion, leave very early (around 6.30am) or wait until after 9am.

The scenery of the southern Wairarapa region is rugged and dramatic. Rolling tablelands end abruptly to form high, textured cliffs. The Rimutaka Ranges cast shadows over Lake Wairarapa, and, to the north, the Tararua Ranges tower over fertile plains. At the centre of this is Martinborough, a town internationally recognised for its pinot noir.

Wellington to Featherston

From the railway station on Bunny Street, **Wellington ❶**, Turn left onto Waterloo

Quay, drive past the Westpac Stadium and follow signs to the Wellington–Hutt motorway, skirting Wellington Harbour's western edge. Pass through Lower Hutt, Stokes Valley and Upper Hutt, from where SH2 begins its windy climb over the Rimutaka Ranges. Stop at the top for views of the range's bush-clad hills and the plains of the Wairarapa beyond.

FEATHERSTON

A 16km (10-mile) drive brings you to **Featherston ❷**, the cycling hub for the region. Pick up trail information from the **i-SITE Visitor Centre** (www.wairarapanz. com; daily 10am–1pm) on Fitzherbert Street. On the corner of Fitzherbert and Lyon is Featherston's main attraction, the **Fell Engine Museum** (www.fellmuseum. org.nz; Mon–Fri 10am–2.30pm, Sat–Sun 10am–4pm; charge), home to the world's only Fell locomotive.

GREYTOWN

A further 11km (7-mile) drive brings you to **Greytown ❸**, New Zealand's first planned

Grape harvest time

inland town. Despite its name, it's anything but colourless and its main street is lined with fine examples of early wooden Victorian architecture. Browse the boutiques, where you can buy anything from an 18th-century chair and Italian earrings to designer clothes and local art. **Main Street Deli**, see ①, is good for coffee or an early lunch; alternatively, try **Salute**, see ②, across the road.

The **Cobblestones Museum** (169 Main Street; daily 10am–4pm; charge) provides a fascinating insight into the region's past, including Greytown's first Methodist church (1868), a 100-year-old threshing machine, the Mangapakeha school (a single-teacher school, opened in 1902), and atmospheric old coaching stables (1857).

While you're exploring Greytown, look out for the enormous eucalyptus tree outside St Luke's Church, on Main Street. The story goes that Samuel Oates brought the first wheeled vehicle (a wheelbarrow) over the Rimutakas 150 years ago, bearing a cargo of seedlings. Three seedlings 'disappeared' in Greytown, and the results are easy to spot.

MARTINBOROUGH

No visit to the Wairarapa complete without paying a visit to **Martinborough** ④, the hub of the wine industry, a short drive from Greytown (drive south down Greytown's Main Street and veer left off SH2). You'll pass several vineyards on the way into Martinborough, as well as the local **i-SITE Visitor Centre** (18 Kitchener Street; www.wairarapanz.com; Mon–Fri 9am–5pm, Sat–Sun 10am–4pm).

Wine tours

With so many vineyards to choose from, the **Martinborough Wine Centre** (6 Kitchener Street; www.martinborough winecentre.co.nz; daily 10am–5pm; free), in the centre of the town, is a good place to start. Here, you can sample a variety of wines from local vineyards

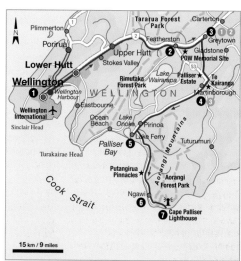

Fine chocolates in Greytown

Cape Palliser Lighthouse

and grab a copy of the Wairarapa and Martinborough wine trail map.

There are around 24 wineries within walking distance of the centre, including **Palliser Estate** (Kitchener Street; www.palliser.co.nz; Mon–Fri 10.30am–4pm, Sat–Sun 10.30am–5pm) and **Te Kairanga** (Martins Road; www.tkwine.co.nz; Wed–Sun 11am–4pm). Hold out for lunch at **Aurelia**, see ③, on Dry River Road, southeast of Martinborough.

TOWARDS LAKE FERRY

Spend your remaining time wisely – sampling wine, perusing local arts and crafts or discovering the scenic south coast. To do this, leave Martinborough and head south to **Lake Ferry ⑤**, a small settlement with contrasting views over the pounding waves of **Palliser Bay** and tranquil waters of **Lake Onoke**.

Putangirua Pinnacles and Ngawi
Continue on, with the sea on your right, to the **Putangirua Pinnacles**, huge, organ pipe-like columns that were formed over the past 120,000 years by heavy rain washing away silt and sand to expose the underlying bedrock.

In **Ngawi ⑥**, a picturesque fishing village at the base of the towering **Aorangi Range**, rows of brightly painted bulldozers park on the beach. The town does not have a natural harbour, so the bulldozers are used to launch fishing boats from the beach. Keep your eyes open along this coastline for seals.

Cape Palliser Lighthouse
Continuing south you'll spot **Cape Palliser Lighthouse ⑦**, constructed high on the edge of a weather-beaten cliff in 1896, and marking the southernmost point of the North Island. At the top of its 258 steep steps, you'll score magnificent views across the Cook Strait to the snow-capped mountains of Kaikoura.

On the return journey, take SH53 to Featherston, where you can take SH2 back to Wellington.

Food and drink

① MAIN STREET DELI

88 Main Street, Greytown; tel: 06-304 9022; www.mainstdeli.co.nz; $
Freshly prepared deli-style food and excellent coffee can be enjoyed inside or out, in a pleasant leafy courtyard setting.

② SALUTE

83 Main Street, Greytown; tel: 06-304 9825; www.salute.net.nz; $–$$
Unpretentious Salute offers Middle Eastern flavours and fine wines. There's a log fire in winter and shady oaks outside in summer.

③ AURELIA RESTAURANT

284 Dry River Road, Martinborough; tel: 06-306 9165; www.aurelia.co.nz; $–$$
Delicious platters, fresh salads and Kiwi favourites, such as grilled salmon fillet, are served on the terraces at the Murdoch James Vineyard.

Spectacular Kaikoura

FERRY TO THE SOUTH ISLAND

Cruise across the scenic Cook Strait, keeping your eyes peeled for dolphins, seals and seabirds. Visit the vineyards of Blenheim in the heart of the Marlborough wine country, and either stay overnight there or return to Wellington.

DISTANCE: 54km (33 miles), excluding the crossing
TIME: At least one day
START: Wellington
END: Wellington or the South Island
POINTS TO NOTE: If you do this route independently (not by organised tour), you will need a car. Self-driving the tour will set you up to start exploring the South Island, possibly by linking up with tour 11. Drive times are as follows: Picton to Blenheim 30 minutes; Blenheim to Kaikoura around 2 hours; Kaikoura to Christchurch 2.5 hours. If you stay overnight, there are good options in Picton, Blenheim and Kaikoura.

Using **Wellington ❶** as a base, you can make a day trip to Picton in the South Island, visit the wineries of Blenheim or join a mail cruise, and return to Wellington later in the day. The tour can either be done as an organised trip or an independent drive.

ORGANISED TOURS

The **Interislander** (www.interislander.co.nz; call centre Mon–Fri 8am–8pm, Sat–Sun 8am–6pm) offers this trip – confusingly they call it the 'Half Day Marlborough Wine Trail', although it's actually a full-day tour. Check-in is 7.40am for an 8.25am departure, with a scheduled arrival time in Picton of 11.35am. Another option is the full-day Sounds Delivery Cruise (with the same check-in and departure time). Upon arrival in Picton, you board a catamaran for a three-hour cruise, dropping off mail and supplies to resorts and homes inaccessible by road.

Picton and Blenheim

Explore waterfront attractions in **Picton ❷**, such as **EcoWorld** aquarium and wildlife centre (Dunbar Wharf; charge), the **Edwin Fox Maritime Museum** (Dunbar Wharf; www.edwinfoxsociety.com; daily 9am–5pm; charge), documenting the history of the world's ninth-oldest ship, plus shops and cafés, such as **Le Café**, see ❶, on London Quay, close to the Town Wharf. Relax under a Phoenix palm, watch the

Marlborough wine country, at the northern tip of the South Island

coming and going of various sea craft or hike to 'The Snout', a peninsula protruding into Queen Charlotte Sound (0.5 hours return), and spy on dolphins.

At 1.30pm the guided half-day Marlborough Wine Trail tour departs from the **Sounds Connection Office** (10 London Quay) bound for the vineyards of **Blenheim ❸**, where you can taste wines from four of the region's top vineyards. The Sounds Delivery Cruise also departs at 1.30pm, from the Cougar Line office on the Town Wharf.

The wine-tasting tour concludes at 5.30pm at the Picton terminal, ready for the return journey to Wellington on the MV *Aratere* at 6.05pm (arrives Wellington 9.15pm; meals available on board). Alternatively, remain in Picton for a leisurely evening meal and catch the 10.25pm ferry (arrives in Wellington at 1.35am). The Sounds Delivery Cruise concludes at 4.30pm and provides the same return ferry options.

SELF-DRIVES

Some rental companies allow you to leave your North Island vehicle in Wellington and pick up a new car in Picton. If you're taking your vehicle across, The Interislander is one of two major companies travelling Cook Strait between Wellington and Picton; the other is **Bluebridge** (www.bluebridge.co.nz).

Picton and Blenheim

When you arrive in **Picton**, visit the

i-SITE Visitor Centre (Lagoon Road; www.destinationmarlboroughnz.com) for maps and information, then drive south on SH1 to **Blenheim**, where you can visit wineries producing some of the country's finest sauvignon blanc. Consider eating at **Highfield Estate TerraVin Vineyard Restaurant**, see ❷.

Kaikoura

Now continue on SH1 to **Kaikoura ❹** on the South Island's East Coast. This

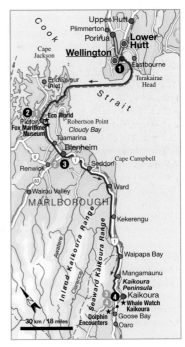

Whales can be identified by their tails

stretch of coastline was badly affected by an earthquake in 2016 which left parts of the seabed 6 metres (20ft) above sea level. 'Kaikoura' means 'crayfish food', and the region has bountiful sea life – sample some at local restaurants such as the **Green Dolphin**, see ❸. The excellent **Hislops Café**, see ❹, is a good alternative.

Whale-watching and dolphin tours
A highlight of this part of New Zealand is a tour with **Whale Watch Kaikoura** (Waterfront, Kaikoura; www.whalewatch. co.nz; tours daily but departure times vary; charge). Trips take 2.5 hours.

Whale Watch is the country's only company offering year-round close encounters with whales (usually sperm whales) and your chances of a sighting are good, thanks to high-tech devices – a sensitive hydrophone tracks the animals' sonar clicks, so the boat can be positioned roughly where the whale will resurface to breath (80 percent of your tour price is refunded if no whales are spotted).

Frolic with dolphins on a trip with **Dolphin Encounters** (96 The Esplanade, Kaikoura; www.dolphinencounter.co.nz; summer 5.30am, 8.30am, 12.30pm, winter 8.30am, 12.30pm; charge). Allow 3.5 hours for the tour.

Food and drink

❶ LE CAFÉ
12–14 London Quay, Picton; tel: 03-573 5588; www.lecafepicton.co.nz; $
If you're craving vegetables order the 'BFS' (Big Fat Salad), which comes with brie, olives and fresh breads – with a side order of local mussels.

❷ HIGHFIELD ESTATE TERRAVIN VINEYARD RESTAURANT
Brookby Road, Omaka Valley, Blenheim; tel: 03-572 9244; www.highfield.co.nz; $$
A vineyard restaurant that specialises in matching fresh local produce with wine produced on site. The menu is fluid, depending upon the seasons and subtle changes in flavours of wine.

❸ GREEN DOLPHIN
12 Avoca Street, Kaikoura 7300; tel: 03-319 6666; www.greendolphinkaikoura.com; $$–$$$
Crayfish, seafood, steaks and pulled pork to die for, just a 20-minute walk along the Esplanade from the Kaikoura West End.

❹ HISLOP'S CAFÉ
33 Beach Road, Kaikoura; tel: 03-319 6971; www.hislops-wholefoods.co.nz; $
Hislops specialises in wholefoods and organics and has an extensive menu with meat, vegetarian, vegan and gluten-free options. It's a great place to pick up stoneground wholemeal bread (baked daily) for the picnic basket, and enjoy coffee teamed with still-warm muffins.

The Municipal Chambers (right) and St Paul's Cathedral in Dunedin

DUNEDIN AND THE OTAGO PENINSULA

This combined walking/driving route explores Dunedin's historic buildings and the Otago Peninsula's wealth of scenery and wildlife attractions, which include colonies of fur seals, Northern royal albatross and yellow-eyed penguins.

DISTANCE: 74.5km (46 miles)

TIME: At least a full day or split into two days

START/END: Dunedin i-SITE Visitor Centre, The Octagon

POINTS TO NOTE: A car is required for the journey out to the Otago Peninsula. There are several fine sandy beaches along the way so remember to pack a bathing costume. Bring sensible walking shoes to explore Penguin Place, Natures Wonders and the Royal Albatross Centre at Taiaroa Head.

Dunedin ❶ is New Zealand's premier university town. Gold was discovered in Otago in 1861, prompting an influx of miners from around the globe, and Dunedin fast became the country's financial centre. Today, the city is known for period architecture, scenery and wildlife. The Town Belt, a 200-hectare (490-acre) green swathe separating the city from the suburbs, is a great place to walk, with heavily wooded areas full of native birds like the tui and bellbird. Extinct volcanic cones shelter Dunedin Harbour, home to an abundance of marine life.

THE OCTAGON

At the heart of Dunedin is **The Octagon ❹**, a little leafy park bordered by historic buildings. Begin this route at the Dunedin **i-SITE Visitor Centre** (26 Princes Street; www.dunedin.govt.nz/isite; daily 8.30am–5pm), housed in the new Municipal Chambers, and walk anti-clockwise around the Octagon to **St Paul's Anglican Cathedral ❺**. Inside, 40-metre (131ft) Gothic Revival pillars support the only stone-vaulted nave roof in New Zealand.

Stop for a brew at **Nova Café**, see ❶, right beside **Dunedin Public Art Gallery ❻** (30 The Octagon; www.dunedin.art.museum; daily 10am–5pm free), which features works by Constable, Monet, Gainsborough amongst others.

Dunedin Railway Station

Continue around the Octagon to Lower Stuart Street. Walk three blocks past the old Allied Press newspaper offices and law

Ornate Dunedin Railway Station

courts to the **Dunedin Railway Station** on Anzac Avenue. Designed by George Troup, this vision of Flemish Renaissance style was built between 1904 and 1906. Featuring a 37-metre (121ft) square tower, covered carriageways, mosaic-tiled floors, original Doulton china and stained glass detailing, it earned Troup a knighthood. **Taieri River Gorge trains** (www.dunedinrailways.co.nz) depart from here daily, some with vintage 1920s wooden carriages.

On the first floor is the **New Zealand Sports Hall of Fame** (www.nzhalloffame.co.nz; charge). The museum pays tribute to a variety of sports including (of course) rugby.

NORTH DUNEDIN

From The Octagon, grab your car and drive north up George Street for five blocks. Turn right onto Albany Street, then park. Explore **Otago Museum** (419 Great King Street; www.otagomuseum.govt.nz; daily 10am–5pm; free), home to New Zealand's largest fossil, and a treasure-trove of Maori and Pacific Island artefacts. The **Otago Museum Café**, see ②, serves light refreshments.

Drive east on Albany Street to the Cumberland Street junction. On the left is the campus of the **University of Otago**, and its main clock tower. Turn right onto Cumberland Street and drive past the historic Law Courts, the magnificent 54-metre (180ft) spire of First Church, and statue of Queen Victoria in Queens Gardens.

If time is on your side, **Taieri Gorge Railway** (www.dunedinrailways.co.nz), northwest of Dunedin, offers an all-

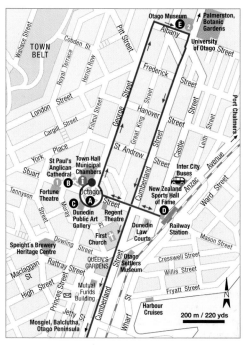

Pull up for a great view   *Otago Museum offers a hands-on experience*

weather activity option, with return trips through the spectacular gorge, riding in vintage 1920s wooden carriages.

OTAGO PENINSULA

The return trip out to Taiaroa Head at the tip of Otago Peninsula, can take anything from 90 minutes to a full day; either way, to fully appreciate its magnificent views, it's best to take the 'low road' out and return via the 'high road'.

From **Dunedin** ❶, turn left at the southern end of Cumberland Street onto Andersons Bay Road, then continue to the Portobello Road junction. Turn left turn onto Portobello Road, which hugs the waterline all the way to Portobello village, at the heart of the peninsula. Stop for a bite to eat at Portobello's **Penguin Cafe** or **Cafe 1908**, see ❸ and ❹, then head to the **New Zealand Marine Studies Centre and Aquarium** ❷ (www.marine. ac.nz; 10am–4.30pm; charge) on Hatchery Road. The aquarium was closed for refurbishment at the time of research, but check to see if it has reopened so you can enjoy the interactive experiences it offers. The marine studies centre – the public face of the Marine Science Department of Otago University – remains open, and 60-minute guided tours of the facility need to be booked in advance.

Otakou Marae

A further 4km (2.5 miles) along the coast at **Otakou** ❸, is a Maori *marae* with a church and a meeting house. Three 19th-century Maori chiefs are buried at its cemetery and the land here is sacred to local Maori.

TAIAROA HEAD

At Taiaroa Head, on the tip of the peninsula, you can watch magnificent northern royal albatross riding the breeze using their vast 3-metre (10ft) wingspan to soar above the ocean. The **Royal Albatross Centre** ❹ (www.albatross. org.nz; daily 10.15am until dusk, tours: from 11am in summer, from 10.30am in winter; charge) is the only accessible mainland breeding grounds of these birds. Guided walks to hides overlooking the nesting sites depart regularly throughout the day. Albatross have nested at Taiaroa Head since 1914 and they share a unique bond with city's human inhabitants; every year when the albatrosses return after circumnavigating the southern oceans, church bells ring for one hour to let everyone know that the birds have made it safely home.

Fort Taiaroa and Wildlife Attractions

Taiaroa Heads also has **Fort Taiaroa**, where an old Armstrong Disappearing Gun, transported here in 1886 because of the perceived threat of an attack by Tsarist Russia, is cleverly hidden beneath the earth. Its 15cm (6in) cannon rises to fire, then sinks beneath the earth for reloading.

Beneath the heads is **Pilot Beach**, where fur seals can often be seen. If

Northern Royal Albatross on Taiaroa Head, Otago Peninsula

time permits, hop aboard an eight-wheel all-terrain vehicle at **Natures Wonders** ❺ (1265 Hampton Point Road, Taiaroa; www.natureswonders.co.nz; Nov–Apr 10am–7.30pm, May–Oct until 4.15pm; charge), and travel across farmland to observe wildlife including spotted cormorants, little blue penguins, yellow-eyed penguins, and New Zealand fur seal pups, all frolicking in rock pools. Leopard seals, elephant seals and orca are also often seen.

BACK TO DUNEDIN'S CBD

At the charming **Penguin Place** ❻ (45 Pakihu Road; www.penguinplace.co.nz; daily tours from 10.15am; charge) you can spy upon yellow-eyed penguins from a network of cunningly designed burrows that twist through the dunes along a rugged, sandy beach. Bookings are essential during summer.

Larnach Castle

Retrace your earlier route to Portobello, but turn left onto Highcliff Road – the 'high road' back to the city. En route, visit **Larnach Castle** ❼ (145 Camp Road; www.larnachcastle.co.nz; daily 9am–5pm; charge), a 140-year-old baronial manor and New Zealand's only castle. It took 14 years to build

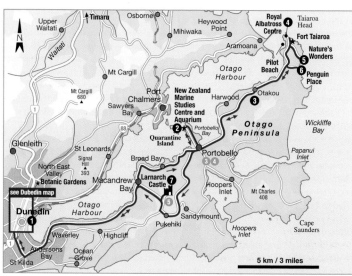

Larnach Castle

(from 1871) and was the home of the Honourable William JM Larnach, who sourced materials from around the world, including marble from Italy, tiles from England, slate from Wales and glass from Venice and France. Most of the castle's 43 rooms are open to the public and refreshments can be enjoyed at the **Ballroom Café**, see ⑤.

From Larnach Castle, rejoin Highcliff Road, which offers fabulous views of the harbour and city, then turn right onto Greenacres Road. Follow this to MacAndrew Bay, then turn left onto Portobello Road, and retrace the earlier route back to the city centre.

Food and drink

① NOVA CAFÉ

29 The Octagon, Dunedin; tel: 03-479 0808; www.novadunedin.co.nz; $–$$

Located next door to the Dunedin Art Gallery, overlooking the Octagon, Nova Café is well known for excellent espresso, delicious set breakfasts and freshly prepared café fare. Open daily for breakfast from 7.30am (weekends 8am) until late.

② OTAGO MUSEUM CAFÉ

419 Great King Street, Dunedin; tel: 03-474 7474; $

Brunches and lunches are made fresh to order here, plus you can choose from pre-prepared cabinet food including sandwiches, filled rolls, salads and freshly made bakery items.

③ THE PENGUIN CAFE

1726 Highcliff Road, Portobello; tel: 03-478 1055; www.penguincafe.net.nz; $

Housed in an Art Deco building and offering stunning water views, this café offers simple well-priced nourishing fare, from bacon butties and poached eggs on toast for breakfast, through to fisherman's pie and ploughman's for lunch. The espresso is excellent, as is the range of home-baked kiwi favourites.

④ CAFE 1908

7 Harrington Point Road, Portobello; tel: 03-478 0801; www.1908cafe.co.nz; $$

Fully licensed dining in a turn-of-the-century building, which first opened in 1908 as the Wainui tea rooms and later became the local Post Office. The seafood chowder is especially good here, and it is served along with a range of other popular New Zealand fare including lamb shanks, rump steak, and smoked salmon.

⑤ BALLROOM CAFÉ

145 Camp Road, Otago Peninsula; tel: 03-476 1616

High tea, light meals and snacks, and other refreshments are served at this café, overlooking the gardens of Larnach Castle. Note that entry to the grounds or castle must be paid to dine at this café.

AKAROA

Spend a day discovering the Banks Peninsula and the attractive French-inspired settlement of Akaroa on this driving route. Take a harbour cruise and enjoy a leisurely lunch overlooking the harbour before heading back to Christchurch in the late afternoon.

DISTANCE: 168km (104 miles) return
TIME: A full day
START/END: Christchurch
POINTS TO NOTE: You will need a car for this tour. If you leave early, there will be time to go to Christchurch via Summit Road, Diamond Harbour and Lyttelton, a scenic route that completes a loop around the Banks Peninsula.

Located around 80km (50 miles) from Christchurch, where this route starts, the little settlement of Akaroa began its European life in 1838, when a French whaler, Captain Jean-François Langlois, landed on its shores and bought – or so he thought – Banks Peninsula from the Maori. Sixty-three settlers set out from France on the *Comte de Paris* to create a South Seas outpost. But they arrived in 1840 to find the Union Jack flying. Pipped at the colonial post, the French settlers nevertheless stayed. They planted poplars from Normandy, named streets after places in their home country and grew grapes,

but by 1843 they were outnumbered by the English.

The French dream lingers on, though, and has been brushed up for visitors. Little streets, with names such as Rue Lavaud and Rue Jolie, wind up the hill from the harbour front. A charming colonial style predominates, and has been protected by town-planning rules.

CHRISTCHURCH TO BARRY'S BAY

From Moorhouse Avenue in central **Christchurch ❶**, head west to where it connects with a corner of Hagley Park. Follow the sign left into Lincoln Road, over the railway line and out on to what becomes SH75, travelling through the farmlands of Halswell, Taitapu and Motukarara.

Here the road travels alongside Lake Ellesmere (Te Waihora) – a wide, shallow coastal lagoon that attracts game birds and waterfowl – before taking a sharp turn left at the turn-off for **Birdlings Flat**. Take a short sidetrip here out to the beach, where the ocean

Panoramic view of Akaroa Harbour

transforms stones such as rose quartz into polished gems, and deposits them on the stony beach, ready to fossick.

Back on SH75 continue past picturesque Lake Forsyth to the small settlement of **Little River ②**, once a notable stop on the old railway line through this part of the Banks Peninsula.

The road climbs steeply out of Cooptown up to **Hilltop ③** and the Hilltop Tavern, where the car park offers grand views over the Onawe Peninsula, which extends into the Akaroa Harbour. This was the site of a Maori *pa* (fortified village), built in 1831 by the Ngai Tahu people to stave off a northern tribe.

Descend into **Barry's Bay ④**, and stop at **Barry's Bay Cheese** (Main Road, Barry's Bay; www.barrysbaycheese. co.nz; daily 9am–5pm; free) to sample their traditionally handcrafted products and observe the cheese-making process (this is the last surviving remnant of a once-thriving cheese making industry on the Banks Peninsula).

AKAROA

Travel on through Duvauchelle and Takamatua to **Akaroa ⑤**, park and walk along Rue Lavaud. **Akaroa Museum** (daily 10.30am–4.30pm; charge), on the corner of Rue Lavaud and Rue Balguerie, boasts Maori *taonga* (treasures), as well as relics from Akaroa's whaling past. A 20-minute audiovisual relates the complete history of the town. The museum also incorporates several of the town's important historical buildings, including the Customs House at Daly's Wharf and the **Langlois-Eteveneaux Cottage**, one of the oldest buildings in Canterbury.

After visiting the museum, walk along Rue Balguerie to **St Patrick's Church**, built in 1863, then continue on up Rue Balgueri to Settlers Hill, where a track will lead you to L'Aube Hill Reserve and the **Old French Cemetery**, the first consecrated burial ground in Canterbury.

Sheep farmer and his flock near Akaroa

Alternatively, you can drive the same route and park near the **Akaroa Wharf**, a popular place for fishing. For refreshments, try **L'Escargot Rouge**, see ❶.

Akaroa Harbour

It is now time to head for **Akaroa Harbour**. Sign up at the wharf for a harbour cruise aboard **Black Cat Cruises** (www.blackcat.co.nz; daily Nov–Apr 11am and 1.30pm, May–Oct 1.30pm; charge), which explores Akaroa's deep, sea-filled crater.

On the two-hour trip to the headlands you will visit a salmon farm and spot dolphins, fur seals and a variety of sea birds, such as the little blue penguin. The company also provides the only opportunity in New Zealand to swim with the Hector's (or New Zealand) dolphin (Nov–Apr 6am, 8.30am, 11.30am, 1.30pm, 3.30pm, May–Oct 11.30am). This is one of the world's smallest and rarest dolphin species, with a total population of around 6,000–7,000 animals.

After the cruise, if the timing's right, take time out to sample the fresh catch of the day and the excellent local wines at cafés, including **Bully Hayes Restaurant and Bar**, see ❼, by the waterfront.

BACK TO CHRISTCHURCH

To head back to Christchurch, there are two options: either retrace your route through Little River, Motukarara, Taitapu and Halswell or, for a two-hour scenic drive of Banks Peninsula, go back to Christchurch via the port township of **Lyttelton** ❻.

For the route through Lyttelton, take the signposted Summit Road, which offers gorgeous scenic views, but travels along an unsealed road with some sheer drop-offs. This route is not recommended for the nervous; nevertheless, those who do take it will be well rewarded visually. Depart with a near-full tank of petrol and follow the signs through the peaceful seaside settlements of Pigeon Bay, Diamond Harbour and Governor's Bay, and on through the Lyttelton tunnel back to Christchurch city centre.

Food and drink

❶ L'ESCARGOT ROUGE

67 Beach Road, Akaroa; tel: 03-304 8774; $

Otherwise known as Akaroa's famous Deli to Go, L'Escargot Rouge dishes up delicious deli fare with a French twist… naturally. You will need to be there early, as its apricot custard Danish and pain au chocolat sell out fast.

❷ BULLY HAYES RESTAURANT AND BAR

57 Beach Road; 03-304 7533; www.bullyhayes.co.nz; $$

Reliable all-year, all-day option, serving generous plates of good hearty food. Breakfasts are huge, and if you're eating later, the seafood chowder and oysters are both recommended.

Relaxing in Hanmer Springs pools

HANMER SPRINGS

This route heads north of Christchurch through the farmland of the Canterbury Plains to the hot-springs resort of Hanmer. Visit Thrillseekers' Canyon, climb Conical Hill, walk the forests and enjoy a soak in the thermal pools.

DISTANCE: 266km (165 miles)
TIME: A full day
START: Christchurch
END: Hanmer Springs
POINTS TO NOTE: This route can be done as a day tour from Christchurch or linked with the West Coast route.

The alpine resort township of Hanmer Springs is located in the foothills of the Southern Alps, 135km (84 miles) north of Christchurch. Surrounded by vast indigenous forests in a landscape cut by sometimes meandering, sometimes roaring rivers. Driving nonstop to Hanmer Springs will take two hours, but take time en route to explore Waipara Valley's vineyards; here, pinot noir, riesling, chardonnay and sauvignon blanc grapes thrive in a warm microclimate.

TOWARDS WAIPARA

From central **Christchurch ❶**, travel north up Colombo Street to the intersection at Bealey Avenue. Turn right onto Bealey Avenue, then turn left onto Sherborne Street (SH74); follow this to Belfast, where it continues as SH1. Soon after you will cross the wide shingle riverbed of the Waimakariri River, followed by the Ashley and Kowai rivers.

Cafés and wineries
Approximately 6km (4 miles) beyond **Amberley** – home to **Brew Moon**, see ❶, if you need a pit stop – look out for the regimented rows of grapevines that mark the beginning of the Waipara Valley wine region, around **Waipara ❷**. A good option for breaking your journey is the **Waipara Hills Café** Hills Café (former Mudhouse Winery), see ❷, 8km (5 miles) north of Amberley.

For a more personal experience, follow the signposts to the highly acclaimed boutique winery of **Pegasus Bay**, see ❸, where you have a good chance of meeting the passionate winemakers themselves.

WAIKARI

Return to Waipara Junction just beyond the Waipara Bridge and turn off onto SH7

(signposted to Lewis Pass). Drive through the birch-lined **Weka Pass** to **Waikari** ❸, the boarding point for the historic Weka Pass Railway, and access point for nearby Maori Cave Art. Also of interest midway between Waikari and the township of Culverden is the historic **Hurunui Hotel**, see ❶. Built in 1868 to accommodate weary drovers, it has a peaceful garden bar and traditional pub atmosphere.

Look out for St Andrew's Church as you drive through **Culverden** ❹. At Waiau River, you may spot anglers.

HANMER SPRINGS

About 126km (78 miles) from Christchurch is the SH7A turn-off to **Hanmer Springs** ❺. During a walk here you can see dramatic views of Waiau River plunging through Thrillseekers' Canyon.

A stroll leads to the 140-year-old single-lane **Waiau Ferry Bridge**, where it quickly becomes clear how this gorge got its name, as bungy-jumpers leap into the fast-flowing Waiau River. Jet-boat rides and whitewater rafting trips are on offer too, (**Thrillseekers**; Ferry Bridge; www. thrillseekers.co.nz; charge). Continue to Hanmer, about 8km (5 miles) up the road.

In town, stop at the Hurunui **i-SITE Visitor Centre** (42 Amuri Avenue West; www. visithurunui.com; daily 9.30am–5pm), adjacent to the Hanmer Springs Thermal Resort's hot pools.

For fine views over the Hanmer Basin, walk the half-hour **Zig-Zag Track up** Conical Hill, just behind the township. Han-

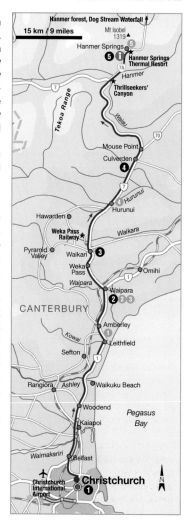

An actual kiwi

mer has other good hiking trails, ranging from 20 minutes to two hours. The energetic will enjoy the Mount Isobel Track, a six-hour return hike through larches and subalpine scrub to the summit. The five-and-a-half-hour journey to Dog Stream Waterfall is also popular.

Hot springs
Alternatively, soak in the hot pools at **Hanmer Springs Thermal Resort & Spa** (Amuri Avenue; www.hanmersprings. co.nz; daily 10am–9pm; charge), just east of the visitor centre. The springs were first used by Maori stopping en route to the West Coast to collect *pounamu* (jade). After the pools were 'discovered' by Europeans in 1859, the first iron bathing shed was erected in 1879. There are now seven open-air thermal pools, three sulphur pools and four private pools, plus therapeutic massage and beauty treatments. Grab a bite at the **Hanmer Springs Bakery**, see ⑤, then either retrace your way to Christchurch, or continue through the beech-covered slopes of the Lewis Pass to link up with the West Coast tour (see page 88).

Food and drink

① BREW MOON CAFÉ AND BREWERY
150 Ashworths Road; tel: 03-314 8030; www.brewmooncafe.co.nz; $$
Great grub, paired with recommended ales, such as the Amberley Pale, all brewed on site.

② WAIPARA HILLS CAFÉ
780 Glasnevin Road (SH1), Waipara; tel: 03-314 6900; www.waiparahillswines.co.nz; $–$$
Licensed café serving a delicious selection of meat, fish and seafood dishes, including great sharing platters, plus freshly baked cakes and muffins.

③ PEGASUS BAY WINERY
Stockgrove Road, Waipara; tel: 03-314 6869; www.pegasusbay.com; $$$
This family-owned operation is one of New Zealand's finest boutique wineries. Its sauvignon semillon, riesling, chardonnay, pinot noir and cabernet/merlot can be sampled at the tasting bar or matched to the menu, which uses local ingredients. Char-grilled Angus/Hereford beef fillet is offered with the vineyard's premium pinot noir. Recommended.

④ HURUNUI HOTEL
1224 Karaka Road (SH7), Culverden; tel: 03-314 4207; www.hurunuihotel.co.nz; $
A cosy and friendly family-run pub with an all-day bar menu. Game pies are a speciality and home-style meals available Thursday to Sunday with pizza on Wednesday only.

⑤ HAMNER SPRINGS BAKERY
16 Conical Hill Road, Hanmer Springs; tel: 03-315 7714; wwwhanmerbakery.co.nz; $
Freshly made sandwiches, rolls and pies, plus great home-baking such as Eccles cakes and enormous chocolate chip cookies.

Shipping Container Mall

CHRISTCHURCH TO QUEENSTOWN

A multi-day trip from Christchurch to Queenstown via Aoraki/Mount Cook. Overnight in the national park, enjoy a flight over the Tasman Glacier and Southern Alps, then continue through the Mackenzie Country to Queenstown.

DISTANCE: 491km (305 miles)
TIME: Two to three days
START: Christchurch
END: Queenstown
POINTS TO NOTE: You need a car for this route. The drive from Christchurch to Aoraki/Mount Cook covers 331km (206 miles) and will take five to six hours, including stops. From Aoraki/Mount Cook it's 262km (163 miles) to Queenstown, another three- to four-hour drive. The scenery, however, more than compensates.

CHRISTCHURCH

Major earthquakes in September 2010 and February 2011 changed the face of **Christchurch ❶**, and the South Island's once-pretty city is still scarred. The 2011 quake killed 185 people and irreparably damaged over 70 percent of Christchurch's buildings. Yet, from the rubble, a brave new city has emerged – a place well worth visiting to experience the energy and imagi-

nation being generated by a population reinventing their hometown.

Within months of the earthquakes, the Re:START movement oversaw the creation of the famous **Shipping Container Mall** (www.restart.org.nz), where retailers set up shop in big metal transport containers. What began as a temporary emergency response measure became a well-loved semi-permanent local institution, selling everything from good coffee to outdoor gear and designer threads. Other ostensibly temporary initiatives, such as the **Cardboard Cathedral ❹** (Transitional Cathedral; 234 Hereford Street; www.cardboardcathedral.org.nz; free), have been similarly embraced.

The **Botanic Gardens ❷**, **Antigua Boat Sheds ❸** (2 Cambridge Terrace; charge for boat and bike hire) and **Cathedral Square ❹** (complete with dramatically ruined cathedral), are now open again. **Canterbury Museum ❺** (Rolleston Avenue; www.canterbury-museum.com; free) has a special exhibition dedicated to the disaster called

Cardboard Cathedral
Punting on Christchurch's Avon River

Quake City 🄵 (after relocation at 299 Durham Street; www.quakecity.co.nz; daily 10am–5pm; charge), which tells the staggering story of events on 22 February 2011, employing interactive exhibits, real-time recordings and using real bits of architecture displaced from where they once stood. No visitor to Christchurch should miss this. At the head of Cashel Mall, the **Bridge of Remembrance** 🄶 was repaired following the earthquake and reopened on ANZAC Day 2016.

Other landmarks are being rebuilt, including the **Centre of Contemporary Art** 🄷 (66 Gloucester Street; www.coca.org.nz), **Isaac Theatre Royal** 🄸 (145 Gloucester Street; www.isaactheatreroyal.co.nz), the **Arts Centre** 🄹 (301 Montreal Street; www.artscentre.org.nz; due to reopen by 2019) and the **Christchurch**

Art Gallery 🄺 (corner of Worcester Boulevard and Montreal Street; www.christchurchartgallery.org.nz).

Pop-up cafés and bars reigned supreme for a few years, but more permanent watering holes and eating establishments are now putting down roots. We recommend grabbing breakfast at **C1 Expresso**, see ❶, before hitting the road to Queenstown.

Leaving town, head south on SH1, through the plains of South Canterbury – a colourful patchwork of fields flanked by the dramatic peaks of the Southern Alps – and across the Rakaia River, via New Zealand's longest bridge.

Drive through Ashburton, then take the turn-off on to SH79 shortly after crossing the Rangitata River, where kayakers and rafters negotiate wild water.

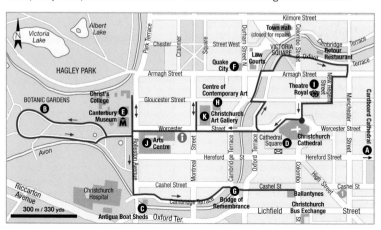

GERALDINE AND FAIRLIE

Geraldine ❷, on the banks of Waihi River, is a hive of creativity and boutique cuisine. Treat your tastebuds at Talbot Forest Cheese (Four Peaks Plaza; www.talbot-forestcheese.co.nz), Barker Fruit Processors (Four Peaks Plaza; www.barkers.co.nz), Coco (10 Talbot Street; www.coco-geraldine.co.nz) or **Verde Café**, see ❷. At the Giant Jersey (10 Wilson Street; www.giantjersey.co.nz), gorgeously soft perendale, mohair and merino wools are crafted into stylish made-to-measure garments.

Continue on SH79 to **Fairlie** ❸ – gateway to Mackenzie Country – and explore the tiny Heritage Museum (www.fairlieheritagemuseum.co.nz; charge).

LAKE TEKAPO

Traverse Burkes Pass and Mackenzie Country's vast plains to **Lake Tekapo** ❹. The historic Church of the Good Shepherd is a favourite photo stop, offering grandstand views of the glacier-fed lake. A bronze sheepdog stands guard nearby, in honour of all high-country mustering dogs. Try **Kohan**, see ❸, for food.

Jump in a hot pool at **Tekapo Springs** (6 Lakeside Drive; www.tekaposprings.co.nz; daily, spa 10am–9pm, winter park 10am–9.30pm; charge), or visit Mount John Observatory, where **Earth and Sky** (www.earthandskynz.com; charge) offer amazing tours of the heavens. Lake Tekapo is one of the world's five official Darksky Reserves, because of its min-

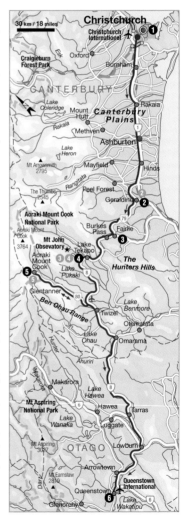

The lakeside Church of the Good Shepherd

imal light pollution. While waiting for nightfall, explore **Astro Café**, see 4.

Continue to **Lake Pukaki** for dramatic views of **Aoraki/Mount Cook** (3,764 metres/12,348ft) across its shimmering waters.

AORAKI/MOUNT COOK VILLAGE

Turn onto SH80 for the stunning 55km (34-mile) drive beneath Ben Ohau's textured peaks to **Glentanner**, where the lake meets glacial river rubble and a vast valley of earthy tones leads to

Aoraki/Mount Cook Village 5. Myriad outdoor adventures await in **Aoraki/ Mount Cook National Park**, from hiking to heli-skiing – the **Visitor Centre** (tel: 03-435 1186) can supply details. Don't miss the 30-minute hike to the Tasman Glacier viewpoint, or a Glacier Explorers' (www.glacierexplorers.com) boat adventure on the glacier lake. Dine at the **Panorama Restaurant**, see 5.

To return, go back via SH80, turn right on SH8 and drive south past **Twizel** and **Tarras**. At Cromwell, turn onto SH8, then left onto SH6 for **Queenstown** 6.

Food and drink

1 C1 EXPRESSO
185 High Street, Christchurch; tel: 03-379 1917; www.c1espresso.co.nz; $
Fabulous food in a very cool setting (check out the sliding bookcase doors). This place was reborn after the quake – note the design of the building, with its in-your-face sturdy architecture.

2 VERDE CAFÉ
45 Talbot Street, Geraldine; tel: 03-693 9616; $
Set behind a white picket fence close to the river, this is a great coffee stop with sweet treats and an all-day brunch menu.

3 KOHAN JAPANESE RESTAURANT
SH8, Tekapo; tel: 03-680 688; www. kohannz.com; $

The cooks at this popular Japanese restaurant know how to make good use of fresh locally farmed salmon. The best sashimi and sushi in the South Island is served here, along with teriyaki and tempura.

4 ASTRO CAFÉ
Mount John, Lake Tekapo; tel: 03-680 6007; $
A stunning view is just the beginning here – enjoy watching the stars appear above the Darksky Reserve over the lake, while tucking into good, reasonably priced fare.

5 PANORAMA RESTAURANT
The Hermitage Hotel, Aoraki Mount Cook Village; tel: 03-435 1809; $$–$$$
Executive chef Franz Blum uses the freshest produce, sourced locally and from around New Zealand to prepare superb cuisine. Incredible views over the mountains. The hotel also houses the Snowline Bar.

West Coast beach

ARTHUR'S PASS AND THE WEST COAST

This three-day driving route provides an alternative route from Christchurch to Queenstown, travelling from the Pacific Coast, through Arthur's Pass in the Southern Alps, to the Tasman Sea. The scenery is breathtaking all the way.

DISTANCE: 754km (468 miles)
TIME: Three days
START: Christchurch
END: Queenstown
POINTS TO NOTE: You will need a car for this route. Bring warm clothes, sensible shoes and a torch for the cave visit detailed below.

The 260km (160-mile) route over the scenic Arthur's Pass to Hokitika on the West Coast provides one of the country's great geographical contrasts. This alpine highway climbs through a visual feast of mirrored lakes, caves and rock formations, ridges and valleys, wide shingle riverbeds and deep gorges.

CHRISTCHURCH TO LAKE LYNDON

From central **Christchurch ❶**, head south on Colombo Street; follow the road for three blocks and turn right on to Tuam Street. Continue to Christchurch Hospital and then drive into Hagley Park on Riccarton Ave-nue. Follow this all the way through the suburb of Riccarton, then veer right on to Yaldhurst Road, following the signposts for Arthur's Pass onto SH73.

This route takes you through the town of **Darfield ❷**, where **Terrace**, see ❶, is an option if you're hungry. From Darfield, continue towards **Shef-field** and then **Springfield**, 70km (43.5 miles) from Christchurch. SH73 climbs swiftly beyond Springfield into the foothills of the Southern Alps, with the scenery becoming increasingly dramatic.

Follow the road over **Porter's Pass** (923 metres/3028ft), which passes **Lake Lyndon** and the turn-off to Por-ter's Pass skifield, before you go past Kura Tawhiti (Castle Hill Reserve). **Cave Stream Scenic Reserve** is about 6km (4 miles) further on, and has a car park with good views of the basin area.

Cave visit
Spend an hour exploring the 362-metre (1,188ft) limestone cave here, with

Helicopter flights over Aoraki Mount Cook offer spectacular views

its flowing stream and Maori cave art. You'll need warm clothes, a torch and a change of clothes.

ARTHUR'S PASS VILLAGE

SH73 passes **Lake Pearson** (pull into the rest area on the right for access to this lake), **Lake Grassmere** and **Lake Sarah**, before meeting up with the braided Waimakariri River. About 40km (25 miles) beyond Castle Hill is the **Bealey Hotel ❸**, see ❷ and see page 113, built when the road opened in 1866 to accommodate Cobb and Co. passengers on the three-day stage-coach journey to the West Coast. It's still an option if you want to stay overnight.

After 10km (6 miles) you'll arrive in **Arthur's Pass Village ❹**, set in a bush-covered river valley among the mountains in Arthur's Pass National Park. On the left heading into the village, there's a **visitor centre** (tel: 03-318 9211; daily 8am–5pm) with displays on local flora and fauna, and a video clip recalling the story of the first pass crossing. There is also information on a variety of walks in the area. Time permitting, hike the 2km (1.25-mile) track known as **Devil's Punch Bowl**, which leads to the base of a 131-metre (430ft) waterfall.

OTIRA

Leaving the village, the road climbs steeply for 4km (2.5 miles) to the pass

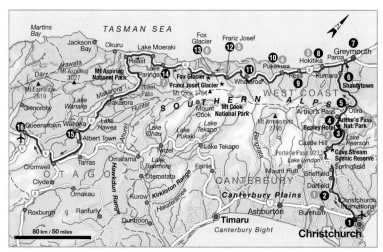

The TranzAlpine Express Train en route to Greymouth

(912 metres/2,992ft), where you can pull into a signposted lookout on the right for glorious views and the company of a cheeky, green native kea (parrot).

From here the road descends steeply via the modern Otira Viaduct into the old railway township of **Otira** ❺. You're now on the West Coast – known in New Zealand as the Wild West Coast or sometimes the Wet Coast; the hardy locals are proud of the pristine condition of their precious rainforests, and the climate that creates them.

SHANTYTOWN

While Maori journeyed to the West Coast for *pounamu* (jade), European settlers came for gold. To see the conditions they faced, visit **Shantytown** ❻ (www.shantytown.co.nz; daily 8.30am–5pm; charge). Follow SH73 through Kumara to Kumara Junction, then head north on SH6, towards Greymouth. Turn off at **Paroa** and follow signs to Shantytown. This replica West Coast settlement has over 30 historic buildings, including a sawmill, stables, bank, hotel, barber's shop, miners' hall, printing works and blacksmith. You can take a ride on a steam train (departs hourly), including the 25-tonne *Kaitangata* built in 1897, on tracks that follow the route of an old sawmill tramline. You can also try your hand at panning for alluvial gold here.

GREYMOUTH

It's another 10km (6 miles) north into **Greymouth** ❼, where highlights include the **Jade Boulder Gallery** (1 Guinness Street; daily 9am–5.30pm; free), which tells the story of this semiprecious stone. **Monteith's Brewery** (60 Herbert Street; www.monteiths. co.nz; charge), is a West Coast institution – take a tour of the plant followed by a tasting.

HOKITIKA

If you're staying overnight on this part of the coast, backtrack on SH6 and continue 40km (25 miles) south to

Historic hotel in Shantytown

West Coast forest

Hokitika ⑧. For details of hotels, see page 113. There isn't much to do in this town in the evenings, except catch a movie at the Regent cinema (23 Weld Street; www.hokitikaregent.com) or admire glow-worms in the signposted dell 1km (0.6 mile) north on SH6. Try **Stumpers**, see ③ for dinner. You can find more information about the area at the **i-SITE Visitor Centre** at 36 Weld Street (tel: 03-755 6166; www.hokitika.org).

JOURNEY TO THE GLACIERS

Don't linger too long in Hokitika though – fill up with petrol (gas), make sure you've got some cash or a credit card (because there are no banks until you get to Wanaka or Queenstown), and head south on SH6 to the glaciers, 148km (92 miles) down the coast.

Ross

On the way you'll pass through the town of **Ross** ⑨, where the largest gold nugget in New Zealand was unearthed in 1909. It weighed 3.6kg (7.9lb) and was presented to King George V as a coronation present. The **Ross Goldfields Information and Heritage Centre** (4 Aylmer Street; tel: 03-755 4077; daily 9am–4pm; charge) gives details on the area's history.

Pukekura

Drive another 25km (15.5 miles) south and watch out for the giant sandfly sculpture that marks the small settlement of **Pukekura** ⑩. Stop off at the **Bushman's Museum and Bushman's Centre** (www.pukekura.co.nz; daily 9am–5pm; charge) for a rough-and-ready insight into West Coast life (not necessarily for the squeamish). Refreshments (including possum pie) can be enjoyed at the **Bushman's Centre Café**, see ④.

Towards Whataroa

Continue another 4km (2.5 miles) past the serene shores of trout-filled **Lake Ianthe**, and through Harihari to **Whataroa** ⑪, the renowned breeding grounds of the graceful and rare kotuku, or white heron. Access to its breeding grounds is restricted to group trips run by **White Heron Sanctuary Tours** (www.whiteherontours.co.nz; charge), who run tours via jetboat, which travels down the Waitangitaona and Waitangiroto rivers, through towering kahikatea forest to a small jetty. From there, boardwalks lead past a series of predator traps and through native kotukutuku, makomako and miro trees to a screened viewing platform, from where you can spy on them.

FRANZ JOSEF VILLAGE AND GLACIER

Shortly after driving past **Lake Mapourika** (famous for its trout and salmon), you will arrive at the village

View into an ice cave on the Franz Josef Glacier

of **Franz Josef** ⑫, home of the magnificent **Franz Josef Glacier**. Your first stop should be the **visitor centre** (SH6; tel: 03-926 2182; daily 8.30am–5pm), for maps and to view its extremely informative display on the history, geology and ecology of the glacier region.

For half- and full-day guided tours walking on the ice of Franz Josef Glacier – the world's steepest and fastest-flowing commercially guided glacier – contact **Franz Josef Glacier Guides** (www.franzjosefglacier.com; daily 7.30am–8pm; charge). There are also scenic plane rides and helicopter flights to Franz Josef and/or Fox glaciers, as well as scenic flights to Aoraki/Mount Cook.

If you prefer to take a look at the glacier on your own, drive over the **Waiho River** and turn left, driving a further 5km (3 miles) into the car park. From here a 90-minute walk along a 4km (2.5-mile) trail from the car park will bring you face to face with this giant river of ice. However, without crampons or strap-on ice shoes (provided on the tour), the glacier itself is too slippery and dangerous to explore on foot.

There's a range of accommodation available in Franz Josef; for details, see page 113. Most of the modern places to stay are located on Cron Street, opposite the **Glacier Hot Pools** (www.glacierhotpools.co.nz; daily noon–10pm; charge), where a series of private and public pools is set amid the rainforest. A good place to eat in the village is **Full of Beans**, see ⑤.

FOX GLACIER VILLAGE AND GLACIER

The village of **Fox Glacier** ⑬, 25km (15.5 miles) to the south, is smaller than Franz Josef. **Café Neve**, see ⑥, is a good option for a bite to eat.

To get to the glacier, drive through the town and turn left on to Glacier Road. You'll reach a car park after 6km (4 miles), and from there it's a 30-minute walk to the face of the glacier. If you prefer a guided tour, book direct with **Fox Glacier Guiding** (www.foxguides. co.nz). Time and weather permitting, take a short detour to Lake Matheson from town, following the signs off SH6 to see views of the summit of Aoraki/Mount Cook and Fox Glacier mirrored in the still waters of the lake. Weatherwise, the early morning is the best time to visit.

If you choose to stay overnight in Fox Glacier, see page 113 for accommodation.

PARINGA

From Fox Glacier, continue south on SH6 through Kahikatea Forest past **Lake Paringa** ⑭ (look out for the excellent **Salmon Farm Café**, see ⑦, if you want to stop on the way) and Lake Moeraki.

Top of Franz Josef Glacier

ON TO QUEENSTOWN

To reach Queenstown there is a lot of distance to cover (267km/166 miles to Wanaka and 338km/210 miles to Queenstown), driving through the magnificent Haast Pass in the **Mount Aspiring National Park**. Keep on SH6 all the way. Here towering peaks surround vast open valleys and lofty waterfalls plunge from steep green cliffs. Make a stop at the spectacular 'Gates of Haast' bridge before continuing on to **Wanaka ⑮**, a pleasant town with an attractive lake and good watersports facilities. From here continue on SH6 to **Queenstown ⑯**.

Food and drink

① TERRACE CAFÉ AND BAR
20 Main South Terrace, Darfield; tel: 03-318 7303; www.terracecafe.co.nz; $–$$
Seasonal menu featuring locally reared meat (Canterbury lamb) and local salmon.

② BEALEY HOTEL
SH73, Arthur's Pass; tel: 03-318 9277; www.bealeyhotel.co.nz; $
Get stuck into hearty pub meals served in a magnificent mountain setting. Kiwi favourites are prominent on the menu, washed down with local wines and beer.

③ STUMPERS BAR AND CAFÉ
2 Weld Street, Hokitika; tel: 03-755 6154; www.stumpers.co.nz; $$
Magnificent servings of tasty food, delivered in a nice atmosphere. Perfect for a beer, a coffee, or something more substantial.

④ BUSHMAN'S CENTRE CAFÉ
SH6, Pukekura; tel: 03-755 4144; $
This wild West Coast café presents an 'amusing' menu of local fare, from tasty 'Roadkill Pies', featuring possum, venison, goat and rabbit meat, to vegetarian 'Grasseater' sandwiches. The owner doesn't suffer urbanites or metrosexuals gladly, and be warned, not everyone will find his sense of humour quite so funny.

⑤ FULL OF BEANS
Main Road, Franz Josef Village; tel: 03-752 0139; $
Very relaxed place with a nice atmosphere, serving a range of good-value snacks, drinks, light meals and ace coffee.

⑥ CAFÉ NEVE
Main Road, Fox Glacier; tel: 03-751 0110; $$
A friendly café/restaurant serving a variety of cuisine, including award-winning beef and lamb, seafood, venison and gourmet pizza.

⑦ SALMON FARM CAFÉ
SH6, Paringa; tel: 03-751 0837; www.salmonfarm.co.nz; $–$$
Sample freshly hooked farmed salmon (catch your own if you wish!) and hot smoked salmon at this farm café.

Bungy-jumping at Bob's Peak

QUEENSTOWN

It's easy to see why Queenstown is unashamedly a tourist town, given its location in an area of spectacular natural beauty. There's a huge range of leisure activities on offer and great shopping. This route – encompassing gondola rides, bungy-jumping and jet-boat experiences – covers its highlights.

DISTANCE: 14km (8 miles)
TIME: A full day
START: Queenstown i-SITE Visitor Centre
END: Queenstown Gardens
POINTS TO NOTE: A number of activities are recommended as part of this route. During the summer it's best to book these in advance to avoid disappointment.

Resting on the shore of Lake Wakatipu, with mountains looming all around and valleys cut deep by swift-flowing rivers, Queenstown in Central Otago is the quintessential year-round holiday resort. It has grown from a sleepy lakeside town into a sophisticated all-year tourist attraction. Within a radius of only a few kilometres, the ingenuity and mechanical wizardry of New Zealanders have combined with the stunning landscape to provide an unrivalled range of high-adrenaline activities. Little wonder, then, that the city is often dubbed the 'Adventure Capital of the World'.

SKYLINE GONDOLA

Begin at the Queenstown **i-SITE Visitor Centre** ❶ (Clocktower Building, corner Shotover and Camp streets; www.queenstown-vacation.com; daily, summer 7.30am–6.30pm, winter 7.30am–6pm; free), which has maps and brochures outlining the vast range of outdoor pursuits available in Queenstown. For a great breakfast nearby, head to **Joe's Garage**, see ❶.

Walk northwest up Camp Street, make a left into Isle Street, then take the first right into Brecon Street, home to the **Skyline Gondola** ❷ (www.skyline.co.nz; daily 9am–late; charge), which rises 450 metres (1,476ft) up Bob's Peak for a magnificent view of Queenstown, Lake Wakatipu and The Remarkables mountain range.

At the top, a walking track leads to the base for an activity that has become an essential New Zealand experience: bungy-jumping. **The Ledge** is run by bungy pioneer A.J. Hackett (www.bungy.co.nz; daily, summer noon–7pm, winter 3–9pm) and offers spectacular views

The Ledge   *The Remarkables*

of Queenstown – if you can keep your eyes open. Speed demons can ride the chairlifts to a higher elevation and take the Luge (daily 10am until late, weather dependent; charge), a thrilling ride down the mountainside. Alternatively, visit **Ziptrek Ecotours'** (www.ziptrek. co.nz; daily; charge) tree hut, near the gondola station, to ride a series of flying foxes which 'zip' between treetop platforms built high in the forest canopy.

CADDYSHACK CITY AND KIWIS

Returning on the gondola to Brecon Street, you can visit **Caddyshack City ❸** (www.caddyshack.co.nz; daily 10am–7pm; charge), an elaborate mini-golf centre, and the **Kiwi Birdlife Park** (Brecon Street; www.kiwibird.co.nz; Apr–Sept 9am–4.30pm; charge), an ideal place to spot kiwis of the feathered kind. Time your visit to coincide with the 11am or 3pm conservation show, and kiwi feeding sessions held at 10am, noon, 1.30pm and 4.30pm.

STEAMER WHARF

Back on Brecon Street, walk downhill, turn right at Shotover Street and follow the road around to the **Steamer Wharf Village ❹**, where there are shops and restaurants, including the lakefront **Pier 19**, see ❷.

The wharf is also home to a variety of vessels, but none so distinctive as the TSS *Earnslaw*, launched in 1912 and affectionately known to locals as 'The Lady of the Lake'. Book tickets with **Real Journeys** (Steamer Wharf; www.realjourneys.

Cruising on the Earnslaw

co.nz; daily, departures every two hours 10am–8pm) for the 2pm trip to Walter Peak.Before then, there's an option to fit in more action in the form of a jet-boat ride. **Shotover Jets** (www.shotoverjet. co.nz) operate on the Shotover River, 6km (4 miles) from town.

CAVELL MALL

Get your 'land legs' back by wandering around the waterfront and **Cavell Mall** area. Although much of Queenstown's architecture is contemporary, some of its attractive original buildings are still standing, including the former Eichardts' pub (1871) on Marine Parade – now a lodge and stylish bar – and the courthouse and library buildings, built in 1876. **Habebe's**, see ③, is a good pit stop in this area.

EARNSLAW CRUISE

As 2pm draws near, return to the wharf for your three-hour cruise on the TSS *Earnslaw* to **Walter Peak ⑤**. On the western shore of the lake, Walter Peak is the original homestead of one of New Zealand's most famous sheep and cattle stations. The cruise across takes about 40 minutes, leaving you plenty of time to enjoy the gardens surrounding the homestead as well as watch a sheep-shearing demonstration and admire the herd of Scottish Highland cattle.

QUEENSTOWN GARDENS

Return to Queenstown and round the day off with a late-afternoon stroll around **Queenstown Gardens ⑥** (free) on the far side of Queenstown Bay. To get there, walk past the jetty and along Marine Parade to the War Memorial, on a tree-lined promenade just behind the beachfront. Beyond, a pathway leads into the gardens. Look out for the memorial to Antarctic explorer Robert Falcon Scott. Circling back, you will gain views of Kelvin Heights, then of Walter Peak. This is a great place to watch the sunset before returning to town.

Food and drink

① JOE'S GARAGE

Searle Lane; tel: 03-442 5282; www.joes. co.nz; daily 7am–4pm; $

With its strong coffee focus, Joe's Garage has built up street cred with its breakfast/ brunch menu.

② PIER 19

Steamer Wharf; tel: 03-442 4006; www.pier19.co.nz; $–$$

This swish café/bar is right on the lake – any further and you'd get wet – and the perfect place to relax on a hot day. Crayfish, whitebait and oysters are often on the menu.

③ HABEBE'S

Wakatipu Arcade, Rees Street; tel: 03-442 9861; www.habebes.co.nz; $

A favourite with Queenstowners for wraps, vegetarian dishes and super fresh salads.

Golden nuggets – the reason for Arrowtown's development in the 19th century

ARROWTOWN

This route drives over the Shotover Gorge, through Arthur's Point and up to Coronet Peak for a panoramic view of the Wakatipu Basin, before ascending to picturesque historic Arrowtown, a former gold-mining town.

> **DISTANCE:** 83km (51 miles)
> **TIME:** A half-day
> **START/END:** Queenstown
> **POINTS TO NOTE:** You will need a car for this route. This trip includes a stop at a vineyard; note the local rules on drinking and driving.

Visiting Arrowtown, 21km (13 miles) from Queenstown, is a journey into the region's past. Situated in a quiet, leafy gully, the town played a prominent role in the gold-rush days of the 1860s, attracting fortune-seekers from around the world. As the gold diminished, so did Arrowtown's importance. It didn't, however, go the way of desolation like many other gold-mining settlements, slipping instead into a quieter way of life and revelling in its beautiful location.

QUEENSTOWN TO CORONET PEAK

In **Queenstown ❶**, turn left at the northern end of Shotover Street into Gorge Road. Continue for 6.5km (4 miles) towards the historic **Edith Cavell Bridge**, which spans the Shotover River. Continue on the same route (it becomes Malaghans Road), passing Arthur's Point campsite on your right and the stables of **Moonlight Country** (Domain Road; www.moonlightcountry.co.nz; charge) on your left, where 90-minute horse rides are available for all skill levels.

Slow down as you pass the luxury lodge **Distinction Nugget Point** (146 Arthur's Point Road; www.distinctionqueenstown. co.nz), because just beyond on the left is the turn-off to **Coronet Peak** and **Skippers Canyon**. The latter is off limits to most rental cars owing to its treacherous nature. Should you wish to explore, **Nomad Safaris** (www.nomadsafaris. co.nz; daily 8.30am, 1.30pm; charge) offer guided tours.

Coronet Peak, a top-class ski-field in the winter, is easily accessible with a fully sealed mountain road of around 20km (12.5 miles). Every July, Coronet Peak comes alive during the **Queenstown Winter Festival** (www.winterfestival.co.nz; charge). Celebrity skiers, sheepdog trials, night skiing and all-

Arrowtown is glorious in autumn

night partying signal the start of the ski season in the region, which boasts four world-class skiing resorts: Coronet Peak, Cardrona, Treble Cone and the Remarkables. But no matter the season, it is a superb place to enjoy wide-ranging views of the Wakatipu Basin.

ARROWTOWN

At the bottom of the mountain, turn left on to Malaghans Road and resume your journey to **Arrowtown ❷**, past **Millbrook Resort** (Malaghans Road, Arrowtown; www.millbrook.co.nz; see page 113), a hotel with an 18-hole golf course designed by top Kiwi golfer Bob Charles. It's your cue to take the next left onto Berkshire Street, leading to Arrowtown.

Buckingham Street

Stroll down Buckingham Street, which has the look and feel of a Holly-wood movie set and is especially beautiful in autumn. Here you'll find artisan stores, souvenir shops and historic landmarks recalling this small town's rich history, among them a monument to Chinese gold-miners. Call into **The Gold Shop** (29 Buckingham Street; www.

thegoldshoparrowtown.com; daily), which sells jewellery and nuggets. Just beyond is a map and information board about Arrowtown, with a potted history of the region.

For a more hands-on historical experience, head to the **Lakes District Museum** (49 Buckingham Street; www.museumqueenstown.com; daily 8.30am–5pm; charge). When your history lesson concludes, cross the street to **The Fork and Tap**, see ❶, or head to the **Arrowtown Bakery & Café**, see ❷.

Further along, located on what is known as the 'Avenue of Trees', is a row of old miners' cottages, Arrowtown's

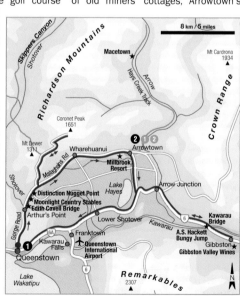

Gibbston Valley Wines cellar   *Hay field near Arrowtown*

library and beyond that the old schist-built Masonic Lodge and original jail.

Panning for gold

If you're feeling lucky, a great way to spend half an hour or so is to hire a gold-pan, available from the information centre at the **Lakes District Museum** (49 Buckingham Street; daily 8.30am–5pm) and try your hand at gold-panning. Just below the village, beyond a long line of car parks, is the Arrow River, where with a bit of time and effort you have a decent chance of garnering a few gold flakes.

Arrowtown Chinese Camp

Another way to gain insight into the hardships of mining a century ago is to walk to the **Arrowtown Chinese Camp** (daily; free), located on the high river-bank, near where you entered town. Check out Ah-Lums Store at the beginning of the walkway and the humorous Historic Places classification given to an old toilet.

BACK TO QUEENSTOWN

There are several routes out of Arrow-town, but we suggest driving back along Berkshire Street and, instead of turning into Malaghans Road, continue straight on into Arrowtown–Lake Hayes Road for a more scenic drive.

Gibbston Valley Wines

For a relaxing end to the day head to **Gibbston Valley Wines** (SH6, Queen-stown; www.gibbstonvalleynz.com), a further 5km (3 miles) along SH6. Tours (charge) are held on the hour through the vineyard and winery, and finish with a wine tasting.

Although the vineyard's focus is on its internationally recognised pinot noir, other attractions, such as Gibbston Valley Cheesery, where small batches are made with flavours changing subtly with the seasons, are popular. You can sample cheese, then purchase a platter to complement a wine-tasting tray and enjoy it alfresco on tables over-looking the valley, or inside beside a roaring fire.

When you've finished, it's an easy 20-minute drive back to the heart of **Queenstown** via SH6 and SH6A.

Food and drink

① THE FORK AND TAP

51 Buckingham Street, Arrowtown; tel: 03-442 1860; www.theforkandtap.co.nz; $$
A casual restaurant serving pizza, burgers, fish and more, housed in a beautifully restored historic building.

② ARROWTOWN BAKERY & CAFÉ

1 Ballarat Arcade, Arrowtown; tel: 03-442 1587; $
An inexpensive range of bakery items, including filled rolls, the 'Arrowtown Bakery Pie', various breads, biscuits and cakes, is made here daily from scratch.

The spectacular Milford Sound

MILFORD SOUND

Last, but certainly not least, this route takes you to the spectacular Milford Sound, located in Fiordland National Park. Cruise on the fiord and return via the Homer Tunnel and Te Anau to Queenstown.

DISTANCE: 598km (371 miles) return
TIME: One or two days
START/END: Queenstown
POINTS TO NOTE: This trip can be done as a self-drive or with a tour operator. If you are driving yourself, note that it involves an arduous four- to five-hour journey each way. One option is to break this up with an overnight stay in Te Anau or Milford Sound. It is mandatory for vehicles to carry chains in winter (May to September), and, as there are no other petrol (gas) stations, fill up your vehicle in Te Anau.

Milford Sound (a fiord mistakenly thought to be a sound when discovered) is set amid the rainforest of Fiordland National Park. Formed from a sunken glacial valley, it's surrounded by steep bush-clad cliffs that rise to meet the Southern Alps. It can be reached from Queenstown in a long day. A number of tour operators, including **Real Journeys** (www.realjourneys.co.nz; charge), offer day trips from Queenstown ❶.

TOWARDS THE SOUND

Leave Queenstown early and travel south along the edge of **Lake Wakatipu** ❷ beneath the rugged **Remarkables** mountain range through **Kingston** ❸, **Athol** ❹ and **Mossburn** ❺ to **Te Anau** ❻, then grab brunch at the Redcliff Café, see ❶. Continue on Milford Road, through the plains of Eglinton Valley and into **Fiordland National Park**.

Food and drink

❶ REDCLIFF CAFÉ

12 Mokonui Street, Te Anau; tel: 03-249 7431; www.theredcliff.co.nz; $–$$
Inspired local dishes, served in a quaint cottage. Great for breakfast, brunch or lunch.

❷ PIO PIO CAFÉ

SH94, Milford Sound; Milford Lodge; tel: 03-249 8071; $–$$
This café serves a variety of meals and bakery items by day, and restaurant-style fare by night.

En route in the Eglinton Valley

Waterfalls, granite peaks and crystal-clear lakes clamour for attention as you approach the 1,200-metre (3,900ft)-long **Homer Tunnel**, a remarkable feat of engineering, and descend dramatically to the shores of **Milford Sound** ➐. Iconic Mitre Peak rises in a ceremonial welcome as you near the end of Milford Road. Refreshments are available at **Pio Pio Café**, see ➋, in the Milford Lodge.

CRUISING THE SOUND

Organised tours include a cruise on the sound, but those driving themselves can cruise, too, with **Southern Discoveries** (Milford Wharf, SH94; www.southerndiscoveries.co.nz; daily, summer 9am–3.45pm, winter 9.45am–3.20pm; charge) or **Real Journeys**. Kayak tours are also available.

Unforgettable elements of the experience include beholding Mitre Peak's three-pointed glaciated slab rising 1,692 metres (5,551ft) from the sound, marvelling at waterfalls, and spotting bottlenose dolphins, fur seals and Fiordland crested penguins near Seal Rock. In **Harrison Cove's Underwater Observatory** you can peek below the top layer of fresh water to spy on deepwater species and corals (only accessible by boat, book with tour operator, see above).

Milford Track

If you have three to four days, consider walking the 54km (33-mile) **Milford Track**, staying in huts along the way. This is so popular it's fully booked for months ahead, but with forward planning and decent fitness, it's a great way to appreciate the sound. Fiordland has the highest rainfall levels in the country, so pack a waterproof jacket. Beware sandflies too. If you're driving yourself, head back the way you came.

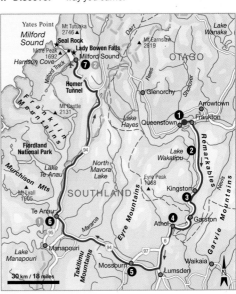

DIRECTORY

Hand-picked hotels and restaurants to suit all budgets and tastes, organised by area, plus select nightlife listings, an alphabetical listing of practical information and an overview of the best books and films to give you a flavour of the city.

Vintage style at Hotel DeBrett

ACCOMMODATION

Accommodation in New Zealand ranges from five-star urban hotels and luxury country lodges to low-cost backpacker hostels and campsites. The country's top hotels are comparable to those anywhere in the world.

International-standard hotels are found in all large cities, in many provincial cities, and in all resort areas frequented by tourists. In smaller cities and towns, more modest hotels are the norm. Motels are generally clean and comfortable, with facilities ideal for families. Many offer full kitchens and dining tables, and some provide breakfast. The New Zealand tourism industry uses Qualmark as a classification and grading system to help you find the best accommodation, shopping and activities to suit your needs. There are five levels of grading from one to five stars. Participation in the Qualmark system is voluntary, so if a motel or hotel does not have a grading, its location and tariffs will usually give a reliable indication of what to expect. Expect to pay surcharges for additional

occupants and peak season. Concessions for children are available. Generally children under two years of age are free; two to 12 years attracts half tariff; 13 years and over, full tariff. If you are travelling as a family, look for motels/self-catering cottages that offer two bedrooms, as these provide good value. By law, Goods and Services Tax (GST) of 15 percent will be included in the price.

Serviced apartments and all-suite hotels start from about NZ$700 a week. Luxury lodges, usually compact and distinctive mansions or custom-designed villas of exceptional quality, offer world-class service and sublime surroundings at NZ$400–1,000 a night. Backpackers are served by more than 250 hostels, some in settings that are just as splendid as those enjoyed by more expensive establishments; rates start at NZ$20 per person for a shared room.

Since much of New Zealand's appeal lies out of doors, camping is a great way to see the country. Many people rent self-contained motorhomes or camper vans; most include heating, toilets, fridges and cookers. Holiday Parks (motor camps) near main resorts provide electricity and toilet, kitchen and laundry facilities. Some offer cabins – for these you provide your own bedding, linen and cutlery. Prices vary according to standards and season. New Zealand also has a number of Department of Conservation (DOC) sites

> Price guide for a double room with bathroom for one night:
> $$$$$ = over NZ$350
> $$$$ = NZ$250–350
> $$$ = NZ$150–250
> $$ = NZ$100–150
> $ = below NZ$100

DeBrett's stripey stairs

with basic facilities; visitors are welcome to park overnight for a small fee.

Whether you're under canvas or staying in a five-star boutique hotel, it's a good idea to make advance reservations during January, when New Zealanders are on holiday.

Auckland

Best Western President Hotel

27–35 Victoria Street West; tel: 09-303 1333; www.presidenthotel.co.nz; $$$

The President is well located and offers excellent value, especially for families or larger groups. Rooms range from standard studios through to two-bedroom suites with a separate lounge; all are non-smoking and air-conditioned. Limited secure car parking is available (pre-booking is essential) and facilities include a guest laundry, gym, internet room and wireless access, licensed restaurant, and dry-cleaning service.

City Life Auckland

171 Queen Street; tel: 09-379 9222; www.heritagehotels.co.nz; $$$–$$$$

Located in the heart of the CBD, City Life Auckland offers a range of rooms, from suites to apartments, all with an en-suite bathroom, Sky (cable) TV, broadband internet connection and minibar. Facilities here include an indoor heated lap pool, gymnasium, guest laundry, restaurant, bar and business services centre. Room service is available 24 hours and Wi-fi internet connections can be found in all public places within the hotel.

Grand Mercure Auckland

8 Customs Street East; tel: 09-3778 920; www.accorhotels.com; $$–$$$

A decent midrange option, handily positioned in the midst of Auckland's waterfront district. If you're lucky you might score a room with a harbour view in the City of Sails – not bad for the price tag. You're also close to the shopping, eating and entertainment areas, as well as transport links. The hotel's Vue Restaurant and Bar boasts cracking views from its top floor location.

Heritage Auckland

35 Hobson Street; tel: 09-379 8553; www.heritagehotels.co.nz; $$$–$$$$

A top-class hotel with friendly staff in a mid-city Auckland location near the Skycity casino and within walking distance of the Viaduct Harbour and the Aotea Centre. The building was once an old department store, and it has been beautifully restored. Facilities include a health club, heated outdoor swimming pool and fine dining restaurant.

Hotel DeBrett

2 High Street; tel: 09-925 9000; www.hoteldebrett.com; $$$–$$$$

There's a retro 1950s feel to Hotel DeBrett, which is altogether deliberate. It's a classy joint in the heart of the CBD, and your room rate gets you an apéritif in the drawing room between 6.30 and 7pm (whether you're eating in the excellent in-house restaurant or not) and a continental breakfast in the morning.

Skycity Hotel and Skycity Grand Hotel

Corner of Victoria and Federal streets; tel: 09-363 6000; www.skycity.co.nz; $$$–$$$$$

The Skycity Hotel is located within the Skycity casino and theatre complex, with its 18 bars, cafés and restaurants and the Sky Tower. The Grand is a more luxurious oasis that includes 'The Grill by Sean Connolly' (see page 115), plus gym, pool and spa. The buildings face each other in the heart of downtown Auckland.

YHA Auckland City

18 Liverpool Street; tel: 09-309 2802; www.yha.co.nz; $

Budget accommodation in a centrally located former hotel building. Sleeping options range from dorms (male or female only available) through to private single, twin and double rooms. There's a fully equipped kitchen, a laundry, TV room and various communal areas.

Greater Auckland region

Abaco On Jervois

59 Jervois Road, Ponsonby; tel: 09-360-6850; www.abaco.co.nz; $$$

Quality accommodation in the ever-so trendy suburb of Ponsonby, a short hop from downtown Auckland, but surrounded by great restaurants and bars. Studio and suite accommodation available, all with free internet, on-site parking, Sky TV and air-conditioning.

Gulf Harbour Lodge

164 Harbour Village Drive, Whangaparaoa Peninsula; tel: 09-428 1118; www.gulfharbourlodge.com; $$$–$$$$$

On Hauraki Gulf, one hour's drive north of the city, this canal-side lodge has a distinctly Mediterranean feel. Country Club facilities include golf course, tennis and squash courts, heated pool and gymnasium. Daily ferry operates to Auckland's city centre.

Mollies

6 Tweed Street, St Marys Bay; tel: 09-376 3489; www.friars.co.nz; $$$$

Even the cheapest suites at this boutique hotel lay on the luxury thick and fast, with antique harps and pianos as part of the furniture, not to mention walk-in wardrobes and big double bathrooms. Easy access to central Auckland.

Parnell City Lodge

2 St Stephens Avenue, Parnell; tel: 09-377 1463; www.parnellcitylodge.co.nz; $$–$$$

Choose between elegant Edwardian rooms and modern apartments near the shops in Parnell, five minutes from downtown Auckland. Twenty-one stylish units available, all with off-street parking right outside. Most units have self-contained kitchens.

Peace and Plenty Inn

6 Flagstaff Terrace, Devonport; tel: 09-445 2925; www.peaceandplenty.co.nz; $$$–$$$$

Set in the lovely, historic harbourside village of Devonport, just a 10-minute ferry ride from Auckland's city centre. Five spacious guest suites, each pro-

The beautiful Waitakere Estate

vide king- and queen-sized beds and high-quality bed linens, plus colonial delights such as deep claw-foot baths, cast-iron fireplaces and polished floors. Gourmet breakfast is served in a sunny breakfast room or alfresco overlooking the tropical garden of palms, frangipani and hibiscus blooms.

Waitakere Estate

573 Scenic Drive, Waitakere Ranges; tel: 09-814 9622; www.waitakereestate.co.nz; $$$–$$$$$

A private paradise surrounded by rainforest, perched 240 metres (787ft) above sea level. The original builder of the hotel, which started life as a family home, had to cut his way through bush to reach the spot where it now stands. The 17 suites have modern facilities, a library and kauri lounge. Gorgeous views over Auckland and the Hauraki Gulf.

Black Sheep Farm

1034 Cove Road, Waipu Cove; tel: 09-432 0435; www.blacksheepfarm.co.nz; $$$$

Boutique accommodation in an elevated character homestead, between two beautiful white beaches. Spacious rooms, all with an en suite and balcony. Ten acres featuring native bush, organic veggie gardens, orchards and rare-breed sheep. Tariff includes gourmet breakfast. Presided over by super Kiwi hosts.

Bream Bay Motel

67 Bream Bay Drive, Ruakaka; tel: 09-432 7166; www.breambaymotel.co.nz; $–$$$

Self-contained one- and two-bedroom units set right on a popular surf beach. Upstairs units provide stunning views of Bream Bay. The motel is located 1.5 hours' drive north of Auckland, half an hour south of Whangarei, and one and a half hours south of Paihia and the Bay of Islands.

Edgewater Palms Apartments

8–10 Marsden Road, Paihia; tel 09-402 0090; www.edgewaterapartments.co.nz; $$$$$

Upmarket self-contained apartments with an outdoor saltwater pool and spa set in an attractive waterfront location close to the vibrant wharf. All apartments feature sea views.

Admiralty Lodge Motel

69–71 Buffalo Beach Road, Whitianga; tel: 07-866 0181; www.admiraltylodge.co.nz; $$$–$$$$

Nicely appointed beach-front apartments, all with views of Buffalo Beach and Mercury Bay. Off-street parking, heated swimming pool, and complimentary newspapers daily.

Acapulco Motel

Corner Malfroy Road and Eason Street; tel: 07-347 9569 www.rotoruamotel.co; $

In a quiet location near the city centre, this good-value motel with friendly hosts has 15 rooms, a thermally heated pool and a mineral spa.

Remote Solitare Lodge

Millennium Rotorua

Corner of Eruera and Hinemaru streets; tel: 07-347 1234; www.millenniumrotorua. co.nz; $$$–$$$$$

Deluxe hotel in the middle of town. Ask for a room overlooking the Polynesian Pools and Lake Rotorua, as there are great views from the balcony. Facilities include a gym and pool.

Solitaire Lodge

Ronald Road, Lake Tarawera; tel: 07-362 8208; www.solitairelodge.co.nz; $$$$$

Nestled in bushland on a private peninsula 25 minutes from Rotorua, this deluxe lodge with ten suites has great views of the lake and Mount Tarawera.

Sudima Hotel

1000 Eurera Street; tel: 07-348 1174; www.sudimahotels.com; $–$$$

Just opposite the Polynesian Spa, this hotel has superb views of the lake and thermal areas. There's a restaurant, bar and private thermal spa pools. Within walking distance of Rotorua centre.

Wylie Court Motor Lodge

345 Fenton Street; tel: 07-347 7879; www.wyliecourt.co.nz; $$–$$$

Standard and executive suites, plus outdoor heated swimming pools set in one hectare (2 acres) of gardens. Restaurant open daily. Wheelchair access.

Taupo

Gables Lake Front Motel

130 Lake Terrace; tel: 07-378 8030; www.gableslakefrontmotel.co.nz; $$

Right opposite Lake Taupo's main swimming beach. Twelve self-contained one-bedroom units, each with a private spa pool.

Huka Lodge

271 Huka Falls Road; tel: 07-378 5791; www.hukalodge.co.nz; $$$$$

Regularly rated as one of the best hotels in the world, the 1920s Huka Lodge is the height of understated luxury, around an hour's drive from Rotorua. It is set within extensive grounds above the Huka Falls, with 20 suites dotted among trees by the Waikato River. Fine restaurant. Wheelchair access.

Suncourt Hotel

14 Northcroft Street; tel: 07-378 8265; www.suncourt.co.nz; $–$$$

This 52-room complex offers a range of accommodation from studio units to two-bedroom units, 40 of which provide uninterrupted views of Lake Taupo and the mountains of Tongariro National Park.

Tongariro/Whakapapa Village

Adventure Lodge and Motel

Carroll Street, National Park Village; tel: 0800-321 061; www.adventurenationalpark. co.nz; $–$$

Accommodation to suit every budget is found here, from studio motel units and standard lodge rooms through to budget bunk beds. Transport to the ski slopes and hiking tracks is easily arranged.

A bath with a view   *View from the Copthorne Hotel Oriental Bay*

Bayview Château Tongariro

Whakapapa Village, Tongariro National Park;
tel: 07-892 3809; www.chateau.co.nz;
$$$$–$$$$$
Completed in 1929, this is one of New Zealand's few hotels located in the middle of a World Heritage park. Known as 'the grand old lady of the mountain', it is renowned for its grandeur, and offers a range of rooms.

Wellington

Amora Hotel Wellington

170 Wakefield Street; tel: 04-473 3900;
www.wellington.amorahotels.com;
$$–$$$$
Located in the heart of the CBD, close to the waterfront, the Amora has 192 tastefully appointed rooms. Its award-winning Grill Restaurant serves a fusion of national and international cuisine.

Copthorne Hotel Oriental Bay

100 Oriental Parade; tel: 04-385 0279;
www.millenniumhotels.com; $$$
Fine modern hotel in an excellent location overlooking the harbour and close to the city centre. Exceptional views are offered from the hotel's One80 Restaurant. Heated indoor swimming pool. It's a 10-minute walk to Te Papa Museum and the theatres, restaurants and bars of Courtney Place.

Wellesley Boutique Hotel Bed and Breakfast

2–8 Maginnity Street; tel: 04-474 1308;
www.wellesleyboutiquehotel.co.nz; $$$
Choose from Deluxe, Executive, Classic and Single rooms at this boutique hotel, where all the rooms are done out with a liberal dose of neo-Georgian charm. You can expect a king-size bed, spacious bathrooms and complimentary Wi-fi.

The Wairarapa

Longwood

78 Longwood Road East, Featherston;
tel: 06-308 8289; www.longwood.co.nz;
$$$–$$$$$
Named after Napoleon's house of exile on St Helena, Longwood is reputedly New Zealand's largest private home. Gracious, hosted accommodation is provided within the house, or in a series of equally comfortable but more budget-friendly cottages. The acres of beautifully kept gardens are well worth exploring.

The Martinborough Hotel

The Square, Martinborough; tel: 06-306 9350; www.martinboroughhotel.co.nz; $$$
Stylish guest rooms, all with different decor, within a refurbished colonial hotel established in 1882. Located in the heart of Martinborough wine country.

Peppers Parehua Martinborough

New York Street, Martinborough; tel: 06-306 8405; www.peppers.co.nz/parehua; $$$$$
Around 75 minutes' drive east of Wellington, this property offers private and contemporary villas and cottages, all located in landscaped grounds at the edge of the popular wine region of Wairarapa, each with their own deck. All

A light and airy Bay of Many Coves Resort room

mod cons are included, and the site is close to several golf courses.

Picton and Blenheim

Bay of Many Coves Resort
Queen Charlotte Sound; tel: 03-579 9771; www.bayofmanycoves.co.nz; $$$$$
In the heart of the Marlborough Sounds, this is a quiet, attractive and very isolated holiday retreat with a swimming pool, hot tub and massage spa therapy. Kayaks and dinghies are available free of charge, as are wilderness tours within the bay to see colonies of shags, and seals and dolphins.

Harbour View Motel
30 Waikawa Road, Picton; tel: 03-573 6259; www.harbourviewpicton.co.nz; $$–$$$
As the name suggests, every room has a full view of the waterfront, plus a private balcony and fully equipped kitchen. A short stroll leads to the water's edge and the heart of Picton. Friendly Kiwi hosts.

Sennen House
9 Oxford Street, Picton; tel: 03-573 5216; www.sennenhouse.co.nz; $$$$$
This bed-and-breakfast and self-catering apartment accommodation is set inside a historic Picton manor that has been sympathetically restored. Each apartment or suite has its own entrance, en-suite bathroom, satellite television and comfortable beds with pure cotton percale linen. A generous daily breakfast hamper is included in the tariff.

Kaikoura

Dylans Country Cottages
268 Postmans Road; tel: 03-319 5473; www.lavenderfarm.co.nz; $$
Peaceful, private self-contained country cottages nestled on a fragrant lavender farm at the foot of Mount Fyffe. Choice of indoor spa bath or secluded outdoor courtyard bath – perfect for stargazing. Breakfast is included in the tariff. To avoid disappointment book in advance as this is an extremely popular place to stay.

Hapuku Lodge and Tree Houses
Station Road; tel: 03-319 6559; www.hapukulodge.com; $$$–$$$$$
A short rural stroll from the seafront, this luxury lodge features five distinctive designer treehouses, plus a number of well-appointed lodge rooms. It is set amid landscaped gardens and is surrounded by a deer farm.

Marahau Lodge
295 Sandy Bay, Marahau Road; tel: 03-527 8250; www.abeltasmanmarahaulodge.co.nz; $$$
Situated just 400 metres from the entrance to the Abel Tasman National Park, Marahau lodge has 12 purpose-built, self-contained chalets set in green grounds. From here you can prepare for the big tramp, hire a kayak to explore the coast or simply chill out in front of a killer view.

White Morph Motor Inn
92 The Esplanade; tel: 03-319 5014;

Bay of Many Coves is in a relaxing setting

www.whitemorph.co.nz; $$$$
Superbly located in a quiet spot on the waterfront, 20 metres from the water's edge. The apartments here include luxury hydrotherapy spa studios with balconies and sea views, garden studios and spa apartments.

Dunedin and Otago

Cargill's Hotel
678 George Street, Dunedin; tel: 03-477 7983; www.cargills.co.nz; $$
This centrally located hotel has spacious, immaculate and quiet rooms. The Atrium Restaurant serves breakfast and dinner, and the Neesham Lounge Bar opens onto a pretty courtyard.

Hulmes Court Bed and Breakfast
52 Tennyson Street, Dunedin; tel: 0800-448 563; www.hulmes.co.nz; $$–$$$
Clean and comfortable rooms are offered in this beautiful 1860s Victorian mansion located in the heart of the city. Each guest room has different decor and there is off-street parking for all guests.

Larnach Lodge
145 Camp Road, Otago Peninsula; tel: 03-476 1616; www.larnachcastle.co.nz; $$$–$$$$
Situated at Larnach Castle – New Zealand's only castle – the guest rooms at Larnach Lodge feature individual period-styled bedrooms with en suite bathrooms, and breathtaking ocean views. Cheaper stable-stay rooms with shared

bathroom facilities are also available. Great if you enjoy peace and quiet instead of bustling city streets.

Scenic Hotel Southern Cross
118 High Street; tel: 03-477 07523; www.scenichotelgroup.co.nz; $$–$$$
In a central location, with a spacious and welcoming lobby, this historic landmark hotel has plenty of superior and premium rooms from which to choose; ask for a room away from the road as it can be a bit noisy. There's a great café attached to the hotel, and service is good.

Christchurch

Dorset House Backpackers Hostel
1 Dorset St; tel: 0800-367 738; www.dorset.co.nz; $–$$
Choose from a bed in the spacious shared room, or grab a private single, twin or double room at this beautiful budget option in the heart of Christchurch. Run as hostels should be, by a friendly international team, the historic house has great gardens and a lovely atmosphere. Look out for Minx, the resident cat.

The Novotel
50 Cathedral Square; tel: 03-372 2111; www.novotel.com; $$$$
Right in the very heart of Christchurch, close to the now-ruined cathedral, this hotel has contemporary and stylish rooms. There's a good restaurant and bar, plus plenty of modern facilities, including a gym.

Hanmer Springs

Greenacres Chalets and Apartments

84 Conical Hill Road; tel: 03-315 7125; www.greenacresmotel.co.nz; $$$

Separate units in a park-like setting overlooking the Hanmer Basin. Chalets and deluxe townhouse apartments have decks, balconies and full kitchen facilities. Close to Hanmer township and thermal pools.

Vibrant Living Retreat

88 Rippingdale Road; tel: 03-315 7429; www.vibrantliving.co.nz; $$–$$$$$

Relaxation and rejuvenation are paramount here. Luxury suites have double-glazing, underfloor heating, and alpine views from every window. Hanmer's thermal pools, boutiques and restaurants are a 10-minute walk away.

Lake Tekapo

Peppers Bluewater Resort

SH8, Lake Tekapo; tel: 03-680 7000; www.peppers.co.nz/Bluewater; $$$$

Lake Tekapo village is finally turning around to face the beautiful water on its doorstep, and the Bluewater Resort, while being on the opposite side of the road, has good views across the lake towards the Southern Alps. You have a choice of hotel rooms and villas here, and the Rakinui Restaurant serves a great meal.

Aoraki Mount Cook

The Hermitage Hotel

Terrace Road, Aoraki Mount Cook Village; tel: 03-435 1809; www.hermitage.co.nz; $$$–$$$$$

The iconic Hermitage alpine resort comprises the main Hermitage Hotel, plus the Hermitage Motels and Chalets, offering stunning views of Aoraki Mount Cook and the Southern Alps through enormous picture windows. Facilities include a sauna, babysitting service and laundry. The hotel also houses the Panorama restaurant (see page 87), where world-class cuisine is created using local produce, and the excellent Sir Edmund Hillary Alpine Centre. You can also do Big Sky tours of the heavens.

Mount Cook Backpacker Lodge

Bowen Drive; tel: 03-435 1653; www.mtcookbackpackers.co.nz; $–$$

This affordable option puts one of New Zealand's premier attractions within easy reach of even modest budgets. Here you'll find modern self-contained units, en-suite dorm and double/twin rooms, plus a popular bar and grill, laundry, grocery store and tour desk.

Queenstown

Copthorne Lakefront Resort

Corner of Adelaide and Frankton roads; tel: 03-450 0260; www.milleniumhotels.com; $$$–$$$$$

Four-star accommodation with 241 cosy rooms, many with views of the lake and mountains. Not in the centre of Queenstown but within walking distance of the main shopping area. Shuttle service available.

Copthorne Lakefront Resort

Hokitika

Fitzherbert Court

191 Fitzherbert Street; tel: 03-755 5342; www.fitzherbertcourt.co.nz; $–$$

Located close to town, these 12 ground-floor units offer full kitchen facilities, cable TV, broadband, spa baths in six units, a children's playground and guest laundry.

Shining Star Chalets & Accommodation

16 Richards Drive; tel: 03-755 8921; $–$$

Set among gardens right on the beach and with an exclusive beach walkway, these chalets are ideal for families and couples wanting space and peaceful surroundings. Chalets are well appointed. Facilities include a sauna, spa pool, BBQ area, children's playground, movie hire and Wi-fi. It's near a glow-worm grotto.

Franz Josef Glacier

58 On Cron Motel

58 Cron Street; tel: 03-752 0627; www.58oncron.co.nz; $$–$$$$

Modern apartment-style motel offering 16 ground-floor units. Perfectly positioned directly opposite glacier hot pools. Rooms have super-sized beds, quality bed linen and spa baths. Guest laundry, BBQ, tour desk, Sky (cable) TV and Wi-fi internet.

Holly Homestead Bed and Breakfast

SH6, Franz Josef Glacier; tel: 03-752 0299; www.hollyhomestead.co.nz; $$$–$$$$$

Set inside a gracious old homestead, this popular place offers comfortable upmarket rooms, a cosy guest lounge and alpine views. The hosts can provide helpful advice on local activities.

Fox Glacier

Rainforest Motel

15 Cook Flat Road, Fox Glacier; tel: 03-751 0140; www.rainforestmotel.co.nz; $–$$$$

Perfect for families, this spacious and clean motel comprises studios and one- and (large) two-bedroom units, all with kitchens, en-suite bathrooms and views of the Southern Alps and local rainforest. Just two minutes' walk from town, it's the pick of the bunch on Cook Flat Road.

Te Anau

Te Anau Hotel and Villas

64 Lakefront Drive; tel: 03-249 9700; www.distinctionteanau.co.nz; $$$–$$$$$

Situated directly on the lakefront, this large hotel has a range of spacious rooms and suites, all furnished in the modern style and many with commanding views of the lake. Facilities include a restaurant/bar, spa pool and sauna. A good stop en route to/from Milford Sound.

Milford Sound

Milford Sound Lodge

SH94; tel: 03-249 8071; www.milfordlodge.com; $–$$$$

Accommodation ranges from camp sites and dorm rooms, right through to luxurious riverside chalets. If you have the time, stay here for more than one night; it's the perfect place to take time out.

Finishing touches

RESTAURANTS

You can generally expect a good standard of dining in New Zealand. Chefs have high-quality local ingredients to work with, including fresh fruits and vegetables and an enviable range of freshwater and salt-water fish, game and farmed meat. New Zealand's 'Pacific Rim' cuisine takes inspiration from regions and countries such as Europe, Thailand, Malaysia, Indonesia, Polynesia, Japan and Vietnam. For meals with a distinctly New Zealand flavour, look out for dishes made with lamb, venison, salmon, crayfish, Bluff oysters, paua (abalone), mussels, scallops, kumara, kiwi fruit or tamarillo. Be sure to sample New Zealand's national dessert, pavlova, made from meringue, topped with lashings of fresh whipped cream and seasonal fresh fruit.

Every region of New Zealand has its own gourmet delights. Northland has award-winning cheeses and subtropical fruit. Rotorua is the place for a *hangi* – a traditional Maori feast cooked in an underground oven. Marl-borough offers scallops and green-lipped mussels, Canterbury the best racks of lamb, and in Bluff, a foodie's world revolves around the biggest, fattest oysters imaginable. New Zealand's long growing season and cool maritime or sub-alpine climate provides ideal conditions for producing wine. New Zealand's major grape-growing areas include the sunny eastern regions of Gisborne and Hawke's Bay, Marlborough in the northeast of the South Island, and the sub-alpine valleys of Queenstown and Central Otago. Vineyards are also found in Northland, Auckland, Martinborough, Nelson and Canterbury.

The list below is not intended to be comprehensive, but instead features our top choices, especially for evening dining, across the country.

> Price guide for a two-course meal for one with a glass of house wine:
> $$$$ = above NZ$80
> $$$ = NZ$60–80
> $$ = NZ$40–60
> $ = below NZ$40

Auckland

Cibo
91 St Georges Bay Road, Parnell; tel: 09-303 9660; www.cibo.co.nz; $$$
Tucked away in an old chocolate factory, Cibo does Mediterranean and Asian-influenced cuisine. The well executed dishes and superb service levels have kept it at the top for over a decade.

The French Café
210 Symonds Street; tel: 09-377 1911; www.thefrenchcafe.co.nz; $$$

A bowl of mussels   *Delicious New Zealand lamb*

Winner of many prestigious awards, The French Café serves contemporary European cuisine in a friendly and intimate environment. There's a relaxed bar for pre- and post-dinner drinks and a conservatory room that overlooks the courtyard, where you can enjoy dining alfresco.

The Grill by Sean Connolly

Skycity, 90 Federal Street; tel: 09-363 7067; www.skycitygrand.co.nz; $$$

Pasture-fed meat and succulent sustainable seafood are the key ingredients here – expertly turned on the grill by TV chef Sean Connolly (*My Family Feast, On the Grill*) – or at least one of his understudies. Reservations are essential.

Harbourside Seafood Bar and Grill

1st floor, Ferry Building, 99 Quay Street; tel: 09-307 0556; www.harbourside restaurant.co.nz; $$$

Fine dining on the waterfront, with wonderful views of the harbour. The seafood is super fresh and delicious; try a seafood platter to share – an incredible dish featuring sashimi, sushi, prawn mayonnaise, smoked salmon, scampi, grilled fish scallops, steamed mussels, Thai fish cakes, pipi, cockles, garlic prawns and chilli squid!

MooChowChow

23 Ponsonby Road, Ponsonby; tel: 09-360 6262; www.moochowchow.co.nz; $$

Eating at this super-cool place is like dining at food stalls in Bangkok – a sensory experience to savour. Expect delicious, zingy Thai food and fresh fruit cocktails.

Orbit Restaurant

Level 52, Sky Tower; tel: 09-363 6000; www.skycityauckland.co.nz; $$$

Venture nearly 200 metres (660ft) up Auckland's tallest structure to the highest restaurant in the tower for a feed from a Kiwi-inspired à la carte menu while drinking in 360-degree views in New Zealand's only rotating restaurant. Note that admission to the Sky Tower's main observation deck and the Sky Lounge Café and Bar are complimentary for Orbit guests 45 minutes prior to/after dining. To get the most out of the experience aim to be seated at least 30 minutes before the sun sets.

Soul Bar and Bistro

Viaduct Harbour; tel: 09-356 7249; www.soulbar.co.nz; $$

A place with plenty of heart and soul – and imagination, on the menu and off it. This is one of the best choices at Viaduct Harbour, with fabulous fish dishes and a great selection for vegetarians. Enjoy some of New Zealand's most popular soul food while appreciating the harbour views. Very popular with locals.

Wildfire

Shed 22, Princes Wharf; tel: 09-353 7595; www.wildfirerestaurant.co.nz; $$–$$$

Cake selection at the Sudima Hotel Rotorua

Wildfire specialises in Churrasco Brazilian-style barbecue fare, in which long skewers of New Zealand beef, chicken, pork, Wildfire sausages, lamb, ribs and fish are basted with traditional marinades, and gently roasted over a pit of glowing coals. Waiters serve sizzling-hot slices of roasted meats directly to your table until you can eat no more.

Northland

Alfrescos Restaurant & Bar

6 Marsden Road, Paihia; tel: 09-402 6797; www.alfrescosrestaurantpaihia. com; $$

Family-run business located right on the bay. Excellent value and very popular with visitors and locals alike. Open for breakfast, lunch and dinner.

The Duke of Marlborough Hotel

The Waterfront, Russell; tel: 09-403 7829; www.theduke.co.nz; $$

Besides offering a choice of 100 wines and 30 different beers, the Duke of Marlborough has a fine restaurant, where you can't go wrong with the locally caught seafood – mussels and Orongo Bay oysters are brought straight from the sea to the table.

The Pizza Barn

2 Cove Road, Waipu; tel: 09-432 1011; $$

Legendary pizzas such as the Musterer (smoky lamb, caramelised kumara, red onion, capsicum and mint sauce)

and the Gumdigger (an enticing mix of smoked salmon, asparagus, blue vein cheese, basil and pesto) are served in the town's old Post Office building. Diners regularly drive all the way from Auckland just to eat here.

Coromandel

Hahei Beach Café

3 Grange road Hahei, Coromandel; tel: 07-866 3016; www.haheibeachcafe.com; $–$$

Ace coffee, really friendly staff and great place for a big breakfast after earning an appetite with a swim. Later, try the amazing seafood chowder.

The Pepper Tree and Bar

31 Kapanga Road, Coromandel; tel: 07-866 8211; www.peppertreerestaurant.co.nz; $$

Fresh New Zealand cuisine; local green-lipped mussels are a speciality here. The lunch menu offers good value.

Rotorua

Abracadabra Café/Bar

1263 Amohia Street; tel: 07-348 3883; www.abracadabracafe.com; $–$$

A Moroccan-themed café open all day with tapas and meze served from 5pm until closing. Excellent value for money.

Bistro 1284

1284 Eruera Street; tel: 07-346 1284; www.bistro1284.co.nz; $$–$$$

Attractively set in a historic 1930s building, this restaurant continually wins a range of awards and remains at

Haute cuisine at the George

Fish on the barbie

the top of its game in Rotorua city for its delicious New Zealand and international cuisine.

Capers Epicurean

1181 Eruera Street; tel: 07-348 8818; www.capers.co.nz; $

Voted Rotorua's 2014 Café of the Year, this casual deli-style café serves freshly prepared fare including salads, hot dishes, cakes, slices, sandwiches and wraps, for breakfast, lunch and dinner and everything in between. Highly recommended.

Fat Dog Café

1161 Arawa Street; tel: 07-347 7586; www.fatdogcafe.co.nz; $$

This popular café filled with locals and visitors – including many of the mountain bikes that flock to the fat-tyre mecca of Rotorua – is open 9am–3pm for burgers, paninis and light snacks, and for dinner until late.

Stratosfare Restaurant and Bar

178 Fairy Springs Road; tel: 07-347 0027; www.skylineskyrides.co.nz; $$$

Any dining experience that involves panoramic views is going to be winner, but the food here doesn't disappoint either. Aim to be seated in time for sunset.

Taupo

Café Pinot

56 Huka Falls Road; tel: 07-376 0260; www.hukafallsresort.com; $$$

This is Taupo's only winery restaurant, and serves up mouth-watering cuisine in an exquisite setting of landscaped gardens and Pinot Noir vines. Enjoy one of the chef's signature platters while seated on the expansive patio with panoramic views of Mount Tauhara and surrounds. Sample Huka Vineyard's fine wines at the cellar door adjacent to the restaurant.

The French Café

101 Heu Heu Street; tel: 07-378 9664; $

Authentic French breads and pastries and a menu that even includes snails and crêpes. Not to be missed.

Huka Prawn Park Restaurant

Wairakei Tourist Park; tel: 07-374 8474; www.hukaprawnpark.co.nz/restaurant; $$

The Wairakei Geothermal Field harnesses the power of about 30,000 tonnes of hot water, and Huka Prawn Farm makes the most of the warmth to raise succulent tropical prawns. Tour the farm, fish for your own lunch using bamboo rods, or enjoy a delicious prawn feast while surveying the Waikato River as it begins its 425km (265-mile) journey to the sea.

Wellington

Annam

125 Featherston Street; tel: 04-499 5530; http://annam.co.nz; $$$

Vietnamese French restaurant serving beautifully cooked and exquisitely pre-

At elegant Logan Brown

sented dishes, from summer rolls and fresh dumplings to wok-roasted salmon fillet and slow-roasted pork belly. The elegant décor and friendly staff add to the experience.

Boulcott Street Bistro

99 Boulcott Street; tel: 04-499 4199; www.boulcottstreetbistro.co.nz; $$$

This fine restaurant, housed in a pretty cottage just off Willis Street, has an air of relaxed formality and serves a range of fine fare, all stylishly presented.

Logan Brown Restaurant & Bar

192 Cuba Street; tel: 04-801 5114; www.loganbrown.co.nz; $$$$

One of the city's top restaurants, beautifully set in a 1920s bank, this place does contemporary classics using top-quality New Zealand produce. Book well in advance to secure a table.

Monsoon Poon

12 Blair Street, Courtney Place; tel: 04-803 3555; www.monsoonpoon.co.nz; $$

A melting pot of the cuisines of the Far East, this richly decorated eatery resembles an Oriental trading house. Diners can feast their eyes directly on the large open kitchen where it all happens. Takeaway is also available.

One Red Dog

Steamship Building, North Queens Wharf; tel: 04-918 4723; www.onereddog.co.nz; $$

Wellington's leading gourmet pizza restaurant, with more than 50 wines by the glass and award-winning beers on tap.

Shed 5 Restaurant & Bar

Shed 5, Queens Wharf; tel: 04-499 9069; www.shed5.co.nz; $$$

Smart seafood (and meat dishes) by the water in a spacious, renovated 1880s wool shed.

The Tasting Room

2 Courtenay Place; tel: 04-384 1159; www.thetastingroom.co.nz; $

Located in the heart of the entertainment district, this casual gastropub offers a range of 'tasting plates' to accompany its wide range of beers.

The Wairarapa

Salute

83 Main Street, Greytown; tel: 06-304 9825; www.salute.net.nz; $$

Tapas and pizzas are served with fine wines that can be enjoyed next to a blazing log fire on chilly Wairarapa winter nights, or, come balmy summer afternoons, alfresco under shady oaks.

Picton/Blenheim

Twelve Trees Restaurant

Allan Scott Wines and Estate, Jacksons Road; tel: 03-572 7123; www.allanscott.com; $$

The menu here showcases Allan Scott's full-bodied wines. Gorgeous indoor/outdoor setting fewer than 10 minutes out of town on the way to the airport.

Salmon at Logan Brown

Antigua Boat Sheds

Dunedin and Otago

Etrusco at the Savoy

8A Moray Place, Dunedin; tel: 03-477 3737; www.etrusco.co.nz; $$–$$$

Located on the first floor of the historic Savoy Building, Etrusco offers an extensive menu of Tuscan favourites including a range of pasta dishes and thin-crust pizzas, Italian breads and antipasti, and an extensive wine list. For after, there's strong Italian coffee, and a delicious range of desserts including tiramisu and pecan pie.

Ombrellos Kitchen and Bar

10 Clarendon Street; tel: 03-477 8773; www.ombrellos.co.nz; $$$

This restaurant features highly imaginative cuisine in an attractive, wood-panelled interior. Excellent wine list.

Starfish Café

7/240 Forbury Road, St Clair; tel: 03-455 5940; www.starfishcafe.co.nz; $$

Within a stone's throw of beautiful St Clair beach, this is a popular café for brunch, lunch or a light meal.

Franz Josef Glacier

Blue Ice

SH6, Franz Josef Village; tel: 03-752 0707; $$

Popular with locals and visitors alike, this great café/restaurant offers an à la carte menu of Pacific Rim and classic New Zealand dishes plus staples such as pizza.

The Landing

SH6, Franz Josef Village; tel: 03-752 0229; www.thelandingbar.co.nz; $

For good service, large portions and reasonable prices head to this laid-back café on Franz Josef's main thoroughfare. There are cosy couches inside as well as a large outdoor dining area. People come from far and wide for The Landing's hearty roast-pork dinners.

Christchurch

Bealey's Speights Alehouse

Bealey Avenue; tel: 03-366 9958; www.bealeysalehouse.co.nz; $$

Stylish alehouse serving delicious Southern fare with dishes ranging from blue cod and chips through to slow-cooked lamb shanks, freshly smoked salmon, and beef steaks cooked just how you like them.

Boatshed Café

Antigua Boat Sheds, Avon River; tel: 03-366 6768; www.boatsheds.co.nz; $

Quick toasties, steak sandwiches, lasagne, chips, nachos and burgers are served at this casual café overlooking the Avon River. They also make up picnic baskets to enjoy along the River Avon's banks or under the shade of trees in the park – a fantastic Christchurch experience.

Cook'n With Gas

23 Worcester Boulevard; tel: 03-377 9166; www.cooknwithgas.co.nz; $$$

The atmosphere is casual but the food is seriously good in this converted villa opposite the site of the Arts Centre. Canterbury ingredients and New Zealand heritage foods feature on the menu. There's also a good selection of boutique beers. The Astro Lounge offers outdoor dining.

Lone Star
116 Northlands Mall, Papanui; tel: 03-352 6653; www.lonestar.co.nz; $$
Hearty Wild West–themed pub fare served in a relaxed family atmosphere. Portions are generous and the price tag is good. Try a classic, such as the 'Lassoo of Hog', 'Dixie Chicken' or the super popular towering serve of 'Redneck Ribs'.

Under the Red Verandah
Corner Tancred and Worcester streets; tel: 03-381 1109; www.utrv.co.nz; $
They serve popular all-day breakfasts, and excellent espresso, salads, risottos, organic house breads, sandwiches, muffins and cakes.

Arrowtown

The Millhouse
Millbrook Resort; tel: 03-441 7000/8088-800 604; www.millbrook.co.nz; $$$
A fine-dining restaurant in a pretty setting at Millbrook Resort. Executive chef Russell Heron has won many awards, including the New Zealand Beef and Lamb Awards for Excellence several years running. Open daily from 6pm. Bookings recommended due to popularity.

Postmasters Residence
54 Buckingham Street; tel: 03-442 0991; www.postmasters.co.nz; $$$
Award-winning restaurant in a meticulously restored historic house. Superb food, fine wine list and excellent service. Open for lunch and dinner.

Lake Tekapo

Rakinui Restaurant
SH8 Lake Tekapo; tel: 03-680 7000; www.peppers.co.nz; $$
Locate within Peppers Bluewater Resort on the shores of Lake Tekapo, Rakinui famously presents Mackenzie Country's finest produce delightfully prepared.

Run76 Café
Village Centre SH8/Main Street; tel: 03-680 6910; www.run76laketekapo.co.nz; $–$$
Serving arguably the best coffee on State Highway 8, this café, deli and boutique foodie store is an all-round tummy pleaser in the lovely little hamlet of Lake Tekapo. Breakfasts are epic.

Queenstown

The Bathhouse
15–28 Marine Parade; tel: 03-442 5625; www.bathhouse.co.nz; $$$–$$$$
Located in an authentic Victorian bathhouse with scenic views of the waterfront. The romantic old-world ambience

The Millhouse has a lovely setting

belies the innovative fusion cuisine served.

Botswana Butchery
Archers Cottage, 17 Marine Parade; tel: 03-442 6994; www.botswanabutchery. co.nz; $$$
Cosy, contemporary restaurant with log fires and an extensive lunch and dinner menu.

Brazz on the Green
1 Athol Street; tel: 03-442 4444; www.brazz.co.nz; $$$
A steakhouse, bar and grill with a relaxed atmosphere and a wide-ranging menu, which also includes pizzas, salads and tapas.

The Bunker
Cow Lane; tel: 03-441 8030; www.thebunker.co.nz; $$$–$$$$
This small, stylish restaurant serves simple, fresh, modern cuisine. Reservations are essential.

Joe's Garage
Searle Lane; tel: 03-442 5282; www.joes. co.nz; $
All-day breakfast/brunch; this is where the locals hang out with their dogs and kids, and eat real local Kiwi food like mince on toast with free-range eggs.

Minami Jujisei
45 Beach Street; tel: 03-442 9854; www.minamijujisei.co.nz; $$
Award-winning Japanese restaurant that does traditional dishes with a modern twist. Menu includes sushi, sashimi, tempura, soups and set meals.

Prime Waterfront Restaurant and Bar
2 Rees Street; tel: 03-442 5288; www.primerestaurant.co.nz; $$$
Lakefront restaurant with panoramic views specialising in char-grilled steak and seafood – you can even bring in your own freshly caught trout for the chefs to cook. The wine list features many local Pinot Noirs, and there's an open fire on cold nights. Open daily from 5pm.

Rata
43 Ballarat Street; tel: 03-442 9393; www.ratadining.co.nz; $$$$
Restaurant located in an industrial style of building with a large native forest display. Serves a variety of different meats and seafood. Their beef Wellington and storm clams are loved by many customers.

Roaring Megs Restaurant
53 Shotover Street; tel: 03-442 9676; $$$
Set in a gold miner's cottage dating back to the late 1800s, this restaurant specialises in unique South Island fare such as Marlborough hare, wild Fiordland venison, Canterbury duck, and Akaroa salmon. It has won awards for its European/Pacific Rim style of cuisine. Candlelit dining in a relaxed, cosy atmosphere.

NIGHTLIFE

Kiwis of the feathered kind are nocturnal beasts, but their eponymous human counterparts are outdoorsy types, who make the most of their days. They still let their hair down after dark, though, and New Zealand's urban centres have plenty of nightspots. Pubs are social institutions – every town or village, no matter how small, will have at least one. In recent years, many city pubs have become more sophisticated, with craft beers poured and quality food served. Live music is popular even in smaller places. The main cities have clubs with a predominantly young clientele, as well as late-night bars. It's not hard to find Auckland's nightlife – walk along Ponsonby Road, turn left into K Road, then down Queen Street and through to the viaduct and you'll hear music pulsating from every doorway. In Auckland and Wellington, and to a growing extent Christchurch, activity in the bars doesn't peak until after midnight. Most clubs have dress codes and you won't get in wearing shorts or gym shoes. Auckland, Wellington and Queenstown are busy most nights, while it's quieter in Christchurch until Friday and Saturday nights.

Auckland

Caluzzi Bar and Cabaret
461–463 Karangahape Road; tel: 09-357 0778; www.caluzzi.co.nz

For a unique, unforgettable night out with great food, this is the place. One ticket gets you a disco, DJs and an interactive show by award-winning drag artistes.

Clooney
33 Sales Street; tel: 09-358 1702; www.clooney.co.nz

Tucked in behind Victoria Park Market, this bar is inside a converted warehouse and has an extensive cocktail list.

Danny Doolans
Viaduct Harbour, 204 Quay Street; tel: 09-358 2554; www.dannydoolans.co.nz

Popular Irish bar in a good location with lots of old-world charm. The decor even includes a confessional box and there's Live music every night.

The Wine Cellar
St Kevin's Arcade, K Road; tel: 09-377 8293

Cosy bunker-like space beneath the arcade and a hang-out for creative types who come here to enjoy the unpretentious environment. There's live acoustic entertainment on Saturday and Sunday.

Rotorua

Pig and Whistle
Corner Haupapa and Tutanekai streets; tel: 07-347 3025; www.pigandwhistle.co.nz

Serves naturally brewed beers and has a garden bar with two big screens to

Fabulous cocktails in Wellington

watch live sport including rugby (obviously). Has live entertainment Thursday through to Saturday

Taupo

Finn MacCuhal's
corner of Tuwharetoa and Tongariro streets; tel: 07-378 6165; www.finns.co.nz
An Irish bar with big screens to watch sports and live entertainment Thursday to Saturday.

Wellington

Concrete Bar
Level 1, Cable Car Lane; tel: 04-473 7427; www.concretebar.co.nz
Light evening meals and a superb range of cocktails are served here, in a distinct New York-style atmosphere.

Motel Bar
Forresters Lane; tel: 04-384 9084; www.motelbar.co.nz
Don't be fooled by the name, more vinyl is played at this cool and discreet cocktail lounge than anywhere else in New Zealand. Rather than just one cocktail list, Motel has several according to different themes and eras, which are constantly rotated.

Vinyl Bar
66 Courtney Place; tel: 04-385 6713; www.ilovevinylbar.co.nz
Quirky bar which, as the name suggests, plays music from the '60s to the '90s. Cocktails, beers and a good bar menu featuring burgers, tasty sausages, chicken satay and honey soy kebabs all flame-grilled and accompanied by freshly prepared salad.

Christchurch

Cargo Bar
359 Lincoln Road; tel: 03-338 9107; www.cargobar.co.nz
Cargo Bar was the first of the 'Shipping Container' bars that popped up around Christchurch post-earthquake. It's a cool place to get a quiet drink.

Dark Room Bar
336 St Asaph Street; tel: 03-974 2425; www.darkroombar.co.nz
A pumping venue with live music playing most nights of the week.

Queenstown

The Boiler Room
Steamer Wharf; tel: 03-441 8066; www.theboilerroomnz.com
A groovy cocktail bar with friendly bar staff, leather loungers and music from the 1970s, '80s and '90s. Frequented by locals and visitors in the know, this is the place to see and be seen, particularly if you have a penchant for dancing on tables.

Tardis
Cow Lane; tel: 03-441 8397; www.tardisbar.com
Hip-hop every night of the week played by leading DJs. A small venue that fills quickly, so it pays to go early.

Maori women

A–Z

A

Age restrictions

The minimum age for driving in New Zealand is 15 – however, you must be 21 or over (with a valid driver's licence) to hire a vehicle. The age of sexual consent is 16. You must be 18 years or over to enter a bar and to purchase alcohol. You must also be 18 or over to purchase tobacco products.

B

Bicycle hire

New Zealand's quiet roads and stunning scenery make it ideal for cycle touring, provided you can cope with numerous hills. The South Island's Canterbury Plains do provide easy flat cycling, as does the city of Christchurch. Here bikes can be hired for NZ$19–139 a day, or about NZ$200 a month for a standard touring bike in good condition. Ten-speed bikes and tandems can be hired for sightseeing in most cities, while resorts such as Queenstown, Rotorua and Taupo also have mountain bikes for hire. Rotorua is world famous for the quality of its mountain-bike trails. Safety helmets are compulsory, so you might want to bring your own.

Guided cycle tours ranging from six to 18 days are available from operators such as Pedaltours (09-585 1338; www.pedaltours.com); on these trips your luggage is transported by van to each lodging along the way. If you're travelling with backpacker transport operators such as Kiwi Experience (tel: 09-336 4286; www.kiwiexperience.com), they can usually arrange bike hire and issue vouchers that allow you to transport your bike on their buses when you're not riding.

Business hours

Business hours are generally Mon–Fri 9am–5pm. Most stores and shops are open Mon–Fri 9am–5.30pm and Sat 10am–1pm. Many also stay open late (until 9pm) one night a week, usually on Thu or Fri; some stores open on Sun. In busier tourist areas and resorts, shops invariably open on Sundays and in the evenings.

Bars, pubs and taverns open Mon–Sat from 11am and close between 11pm and 2am, depending on their licence. Clubs usually open their doors at 7.30–8pm and close around 4am.

C

Crime and safety

If you take due care, there is no reason to expect trouble in New Zealand. Take the usual sensible precautions, such as locking your car and never

Unbeatable views on the South Island's West Coast

leaving tempting articles visible inside. Make sure camper vans are well secured when you leave them to go exploring. Keep valuables in the hotel safe, and don't leave valuable possessions on the beach while you swim. Any theft should be reported immediately to the police.

Drugs offences, particularly if they relate to harder drugs, are treated very seriously. Marijuana is widely available but remains illegal.

While New Zealand is a safe country, it is unwise for a lone woman to walk at night in some big-city areas, such as the 'K' Road nightlife area in Auckland. New Zealand has some fearsome-looking motorcycle gangs on the roads, but they are unlikely to hassle tourists.

Customs and entry requirements

Visas and passports

All visitors to New Zealand need a passport valid for at least three months beyond the date they intend leaving the country. Citizens of Canada, Ireland, South Africa, the US and several other countries do not require an entry visa if they intend to stay for less than three months. British passport-holders can stay visa-free for six months; Australians can stay indefinitely. To gain entry, visitors must hold fully paid onward or return tickets to a country they have permission to enter, and sufficient funds to maintain themselves during their stay in New Zealand (calculated at least NZ$1,000 per person per month).

Everyone arriving in New Zealand must complete an arrival card handed out on the aircraft.

Banned substances

Animal products, fruit, plant material, or foodstuffs that could contain plant or animal pests and diseases are banned. Heavy fines are imposed on people caught carrying these and ignorance is not accepted as an excuse. Leave all food on the aircraft, or place in the bins provided on the approach to the immigration area – even if it's something you've been given on the plane.

Drugs, including marijuana and cocaine, are illegal in New Zealand; penalties for possession are heavy and being apprehended in possession of such substances will seriously risk affecting your visa status.

Duty on imported goods

Goods up to a total combined value of NZ$700 are free of duty and tax, but goods in excess of this may attract both. If you are over 17 you may also take the following into New Zealand free of duty and tax: 200 cigarettes or 250 grams of tobacco or 50 cigars (or a mixture of all three not weighing more than 250 grams); 4.5 litres of wine (equivalent to six standard 750-ml wine bottles) or 4.5 litres of beer and three 1,125-ml bottles of spirits or liqueur. There is no restric-

Red-blossoming pohutukawa tree on the Coromandel Peninsula

tion on the import or export of foreign or local currency.

Visitors to New Zealand may purchase duty-free goods, which are not subject to local taxes, from airport duty-free shops upon arrival and departure. Duty-free stores in central Auckland, Wellington and Christchurch can deliver purchases to aircraft departure lounges.

E

Electricity

230V/50Hz AC is standard. Most hotels have sockets for 110V AC electric razors. The country uses Australasian/Pacific-model plugs with three flat pins.

Embassies and consulates

The following is a list of the main consular offices in New Zealand:

Australia: 72–6 Hobson Street, Thorndon, Wellington; tel: 04-473 6411; www.newzealand.embassy.gov.au

Canada: 125 The Terrace, Wellington (PO Box 8047), Wellington; tel: 04-473 9577; www.canadainternational.gc.ca

Ireland: Level 1, 5 High Street, Auckland; tel: 09-919 7450; www.ireland.co.nz.

UK: 44 Hill Street, Wellington (PO Box 1812), Wellington 6140; tel: 04-924 2888; www.gov.uk/british-high-commission-wellington

US: 29 Fitzherbert Terrace, Thorndon (PO Box 1190), Wellington; tel: 04-462 6000; http://newzealand.usembassy.gov.

Emergencies

Dial 111 for emergency calls to police, fire or ambulance services. Emergency numbers for doctors, dentists, hospitals and local authorities are given in the front of local telephone directories and posted in telephone boxes. Police control call-outs for search-and-rescue services in the bush.

Fire hazards

Fire poses a constant threat to New Zealand's natural beauty. In summer, scrub and grass are tinder-dry, and the slightest spark can start a blaze. Do not throw matches or cigarettes from car windows, and don't light fires in restricted areas. Beach barbecues are tolerated as long as you remain a safe distance from trees, but be sure to shelter the fire well from sea breezes – a chance cinder can set a whole bush-bound coast alight. Always extinguish a fire carefully by dousing it with water or covering it with earth. Glass can concentrate the sun's rays and start fires, so store empty bottles in the shade and take them with you when you leave.

Gay and lesbian travellers

New Zealand is not generally a homophobic country, although prejudice may persist in smaller towns. The country has a history of enlightened

The New Zealand bush

laws relating to human rights. Homosexuality ceased to be categorised as a criminal offence in 1986, and the age of consent was set at 16 (the same as for heterosexuals).

There are lots of facilities and activities in New Zealand catering for gay, lesbian and bisexual travellers, including Gay Ski Week in Queenstown and the Great Party weekend in Wellington. For further information, contact Gay Tourism New Zealand (www.gaytravel. co.nz).

Guides and tours

A wide choice of escorted package tours is available. These include fly/drive arrangements (with or without accommodation), camper or motorhome hire, fully escorted coach holidays (North Island, South Island, or both), escorted budget coach holidays, farm holidays, trekking holidays and ski packages.

A scenic flight tour is recommended at any of the following destinations: Rotorua, Lake Tekapo, Mount Cook, the Fox and Franz Josef glaciers, Queenstown and Milford Sound. Alpine flights use special planes with retractable skis for landing on snow and ice.

H

Health care

Both public and private health services are of a high standard in New Zealand. Hotels and motels usually have a doctor on call, and doctors are listed separately at the front of telephone directories. Medical services are not free, except as a result of an accident, so you are strongly advised to arrange health insurance in advance. In the case of an accident, all visitors are entitled to compensation, covering expenses such as doctor's fees and hospitalisation. New Zealand has reciprocal health agreements with Australia and the UK, but not with any other countries.

Insects and venomous creatures

You don't have to worry too much about venomous creepy-crawlies in New Zealand. The only venomous spider, the katipo, is rare and retiring, and there are no snakes. However, there is a flying pest that delivers a painful, itchy bite: the gnat-sized sandfly. It is prevalent on the West Coast of the South Island, so ensure you carry insect repellent if travelling in this area. The European wasp, with its yellow-and-black-striped abdomen, has colonised New Zealand and become a problem in some bush areas. Hikers should carry antihistamine medication as a precaution. Mosquitos can also be a pest.

Marine dangers

Sharks do live in New Zealand's waters, including some species that are dangerous to humans, such as great whites, bronze whalers and mako. Attacks have happened, but they are rare. Far more

Aoraki Mount Cook

dangerous is the sea itself in some areas – make sure you seek out reliable local knowledge before swimming anywhere that there might be rips, big surf or strong currents. River crossings can be similarly dangerous when hiking – if in doubt, don't cross.

Sunburn

Guard against sunburn every day in the summer (even when there is cloud cover) and in alpine areas year-round, by using at least a factor 30 sunscreen lotion.

Pharmacies

Chemists (pharmacies) usually open 9am–5.30pm Mon–Fri, as well as on Sat morning. The addresses and phone numbers of emergency chemists (for after-hours service) are posted on the doors of all pharmacies.

Drinking water

New Zealand has an excellent public water supply. Tap water is safe to drink.

Hot pool safety

There is a small danger of contacting amoebic meningitis from bathing in hot springs and pools in thermal areas such as Rotorua – to protect yourself against this potentially deadly condition, keep your head above the water at all times. If you develop a headache or fever, or begin vomiting several days after visiting a hot pool, seek medical treatment immediately.

Volcanoes and earthquakes

As the major and deadly earthquakes in Canterbury in 2010 and 2011 showed, New Zealand is poised on a geologically volatile part of the planet and even the major cities are not safe from sudden and potentially catastrophic natural events. Reminders of such activity can be seen at the Tangiwai rail disaster memorial, on SH49 between Ohakune and Waiouru. Here, in 1953, a lahar flooded the Whangaehu River, destroying the Tangiwai Railway Bridge and killing 153 people. Fortunately, when Mount Ruapehu's Crater Lake burst its banks again, in March 2007, an alarm system provided a warning, before a torrent of mud and debris poured through the river gorge. Such alarms are in place around the country, and scientists constantly monitor seismic activity, so the risks of any nasty surprises are kept as low as possible. You may, however, experience an earthquake during your stay. The best advice is to protect your head and to shelter beneath something solid such as a doorway.

Holidays

The major public holidays are:
1 and 2 Jan: New Year
6 Feb: Waitangi Day
Mar/Apr: Good Friday, Easter Monday
25 Apr: Anzac Day
June: Queen's Birthday (first Mon)
Oct: Labour Day (fourth Mon)
25/26 Dec: Christmas, Boxing Day

Zorbing

Extra holidays

When Christmas, Boxing Day or New Year's Day falls on a Saturday or Sunday, the public holiday is observed on the following Monday. Also, each province holds a holiday on its own anniversary. These range through the year and can vary, so it's worth checking with an authority such as Tourism New Zealand (www.newzealand.com) before you depart.

L

Laundry/dry cleaning

The majority of hostels, motels and some hotels have self-service laundry facilities. Large hotels provide laundry and dry-cleaning services. At local dry cleaners your clothing will usually be returned to you in 48 hours, although you can generally pay more for a speedier service.

M

Maps

Tourist offices and car-hire companies distribute free maps. The New Zealand Automobile Association also produces regional maps and excellent district maps. Alternatively, Hema Maps, Wises Maps and Kiwi Maps are also well produced and widely available throughout the country. Google has the country covered from a topographical and street view perspective, but remember some images and maps (even those online) are dated – this is particularly important to bear in mind when you're navigating Christchurch, where the cityscape changed dramatically after the 2011 earthquake.

Media

Newspapers and magazines

Mass-circulation daily newspapers are produced in New Zealand's main population centres. *The Herald* (www.nzherald.co.nz) in Auckland is the North Island's largest circulation paper, while *The Press* (www.press.co.nz) in Christchurch is the South Island's largest. A good online source of news can be found here www.stuff.co.nz. There are also local daily papers published in provincial centres and most towns. International papers and magazines can be found in large bookstores in the main cities.

The Listener (www.notedlistener.co.nz), a weekly news magazine, publishes a television and radio guide as well as articles on the arts and social issues. *Metro* and *North and South* current affairs magazines provide lively, informative and topical features. International magazines are widely available.

Television

Sky television (featuring BBC News and CNN) is widely available, otherwise television consists of 10 free commercial channels as well as a number of regional television stations. Commer-

Hiking in Marlborough wine country

cials proliferate on channels 1–3, along with many overseas-made repeats and some local content.

Radio

National Radio is the best station for news, current events and quality programming; numerous other stations cater to all tastes. The BBC World Service is easy to tune into throughout the country, and presents news and current events to a high standard, albeit from a distant part of the planet.

Money

Currency

New Zealand has a decimal currency system, with one dollar made up of 100 cents. Coins come in denominations of 10¢, 20¢, 50¢, NZ$1 and NZ$2. Notes come in NZ$5, NZ$10, NZ$20, NZ$50 and NZ$100 denominations.

Banking hours

These are usually 9am–4.30pm Mon–Fri. Some branches open on Sat until 12.30pm.

Credit cards

Internationally recognised credit cards are widely accepted, and major currencies such as US dollars, UK pounds and Australian dollars can be readily changed at banks.

International credit cards encoded with a PIN may be used to withdraw cash from automatic teller machines (ATMs), which are widely available in main shopping centres and suburban malls. Check with your bank before departure to ensure this facility is available to you, and whether you will be charged for every withdrawal.

NB: Note that 'Smart Cards', which often have no magnetic strip, are not universally accepted in New Zealand, so contact your card provider for further information prior to your trip.

Traveller's cheques

Traveller's cheques can also be cashed at banks, bigger hotels and tourist-orientated shops.

Goods and service tax

A 15 percent Goods and Service Tax (GST), generally included in the quoted price (except with trade goods), is slapped onto virtually everything.

Police

New Zealand police are approachable and helpful, although note that some carry taser guns.

See also Emergencies, see page 126.

Population and multiculturalism

New Zealand has 4.7 million people, mostly of British descent, with the largest minority (about 14 percent) being Maori of Polynesian ori-

Mitre Peak, Fiordland

gin. There is a large Asian influence too, which can be seen (and tasted) in the country's cuisine. New Zealanders are sometimes called 'Kiwis' after the flightless bird that is the country's unofficial national symbol (not after the small furry fruit that also shares the Kiwi name!) You may also hear the term Pakeha, which is the Maori term for Europeans.

Post offices

Main post offices (Post Shops) sell stationery as well as offering postal and banking services. In rural areas the general store doubles as the Post Shop. It costs NZ$1.80 to send postcards to anywhere in the world. International airmail envelopes cost NZ$2.20. Domestic mail is divided into first (FastPost) and second-class (Standard).

R

Religion

New Zealand has no state Church, but Christianity is the dominant religion. Protestants outnumber Catholics. The daily papers give details of addresses and times of services.

S

Smoking

Smoking is not permitted in any restaurants, bars or public buildings in New Zealand.

T

Telephones

Landlines and public (pay) phones

Calls that are made on private phones are vastly cheaper than those made on public (pay) phones. Local calls from private phones are free to other landlines.

Coin-operated phones are increasingly rare in New Zealand, although a few remain at airports and railway stations. Card-operated public phones with trunk (toll) and international direct dialling (IDD) options are located throughout the country.

Phone cards are readily available from post offices, supermarkets and petrol stations; they come in denominations of NZ$5, NZ$10, NZ$20 and NZ$50.

Dialling codes

The country code for New Zealand is 64. To call abroad, first dial the international access code, 00, then the country code.

Mobile (cell) phones

Cell phones operate on GSM and 3G networks, and are provided by a variety of operators including Vodafone (www.vodafone.com) and Spark (www.spark.co.nz). Mobile phone hire, including prepay options, is readily available. It is far cheaper to make calls using a hired

The start of SH1, New Zealand's main highway

mobile or to purchase a local SIM card for your own mobile (as long as it has an international roaming facility) as local call rates will apply.

Time

New Zealand is one of the first places in the world to see the new day, 12 hours ahead of GMT (Greenwich Mean Time). In summer New Zealand uses 'daylight saving', with clocks put forward one hour to GMT+13. Daylight saving begins on the last Sunday in September and ends on the first Sunday of the following April, when clocks are put back to GMT+12.

Tipping

Tipping is uncommon in New Zealand; however, restaurant, hospitality and tourism staff will appreciate a tip if their service has been good. Taxi drivers do not expect tips, and service charges are not added to hotel or restaurant bills.

Toilets

Toilets for public use are found in hotel lobbies, shopping centres, large stores, restaurants, museums, cinemas and pubs. Most towns provide public 'rest rooms'; they are also located in most picnic spots along main roads and at the most popular beaches.

Tourist information

Within New Zealand

New Zealand has an established network of visitor information centres known as i-SITES. These are referenced throughout the routes in this guide.

Outside New Zealand

Tourism New Zealand (www.newzealand.com) maintains marketing and information offices in the following countries:

Australia: Level 12, 61 York Street, Sydney, NSW 2000; tel: 02-8249 4800.
UK: New Zealand House, 80 Haymarket, London SW1Y 4TQ; tel: 020-7930 1662.
US: Suite 300, 501 Santa Monica Boulevard, Santa Monica, CA 90401; tel: 1-310 395 7480

Transport

Getting to New Zealand

From Australia: Frequent direct flights operated by Air New Zealand and Qantas link Sydney and Auckland each day. These days, Australian airlines view New Zealand as virtually a domestic destination. The same view applies vice versa – though obviously you need appropriate documents to travel between the two countries. Qantas and Air New Zealand offer direct flights to Auckland from major Australian cities. Direct flights also operate between Christchurch, Queenstown and Wellington from Brisbane, Melbourne, Canberra, Perth and Sydney. Freedom Air, an Air New Zealand subsidiary, also links centres on each side of the Tasman Sea.

From North America: Auckland is linked with Los Angeles, Dallas and

Quiet roads are typical in country areas

Houston by direct flights, taking less than 13 hours, on average. Several connections a day run from Auckland to Wellington or Christchurch. New Zealand can also be reached with an additional one or two stops in the Pacific. It can be reached from New York City in just two stops and from San Francisco in one stop.

From the UK: Regular weekly flights operate by airlines including Air New Zealand, Qantas and various Asian carriers from London to New Zealand with one, two or three stops en route. Since the journey takes at least 24 hours, the cheapest ticket may not be the best deal – it may involve more than one airline and two or more stops, typically requiring you to change aircraft (and possibly airlines) in Singapore, Hong Kong, Sydney or Los Angeles.

Airports

Auckland (AKL) International is 22km (13.5 miles) south of the city centre. Transfer to the city by taxi or bus (30–45 mins).

Christchurch (CHC) International is 10km (6 miles) northwest of the city centre. Transfer to the city by taxi or bus (25 mins).

Wellington (WLG) International is 8km (5 miles) southeast of the city centre. Transfer to the city by taxi or bus (15 mins).

Long-haul international flights generally land in Auckland. Trans-Tasman flights from Australia also serve Wellington, Auckland and Christchurch, with additional direct air links between Australia and smaller centres such as Queenstown, Hamilton, Dunedin and Palmerston North.

Domestic flights

Air New Zealand is the primary domestic carrier, with Qantas, Jetstar, Sunair Aviation, Barrier Air Auckland and Virgin competing on main trunk routes. A number of smaller companies serve provincial towns. There are frequent flights from the main centres, provincial towns and resort areas.

City buses/trains

Local buses run according to a published timetable. Fares are calculated according to the number of 'sections' travelled. Some city shuttle buses have 'honesty boxes', into which you drop the required amount. Wellington has electric trains that travel to the northern suburbs and Auckland runs trains serving suburbs to the south and west.

Coach services

Coaches provide countryside service. Many are air-conditioned although all are heated in winter. The main national coach providers are InterCity (www.intercity.co.nz and Naked Bus (www.nakedbus.co.nz). Budget-priced backpacker coaches such as Kiwi Experience (www.kiwiexperience.com) also cover major routes.

An Auckland bus

A number of coach companies offer passes along the routes they operate, either with unlimited stops along a fixed line or a certain number of travel days within a set time frame. Some passes include one ferry and one train journey. Discounts of up to 15 percent are offered to seniors, students, backpackers and children. Earlybird fares starting from $1 are available online.

Trains

New Zealand offers three scenic long-distance rail services. For full details, contact Tranz Scenic, tel: 04-495 0775; www.tranzscenic.co.nz. Here is a rundown of one-way adult fares:

Northern Explorer (Auckland–Wellington), from NZ$179.

Interislander (Wellington–Picton), from NZ$56.

TranzAlpine (Christchurch–Greymouth), from NZ$179.

Scenic rail passes are also available; prices for adults begin at NZ$439.

Ferries

The North and South Islands are linked by both passenger and vehicular ferries (www.interislander.co.nz; www.blue bridge.co.nz), which depart frequently. Stewart Island and Great Barrier Island are also connected by ferry, with less frequent daily departures.

Driving

Road conditions: roads are generally good, and light traffic in remoter parts of the country makes driving a pleasure, although roads can be tortuously windy. Auckland often has traffic jams outside of peak hours due to the ongoing and extensive upgrading of its road infrastructure. Drive extremely carefully in winter, when you should carry snow chains – on some routes, such as the Milford Road, it is illegal not to carry them from May to September (make sure you know how to put them on your vehicle too).

Rules and regulations: provided you hold a valid overseas driver's licence or an international driving permit, you can drive in New Zealand for up to one year before you are required to apply for a New Zealand licence. You must be able to prove you hold a valid overseas licence and drive only those types of vehicles for which you were licensed in your country of origin. Carry your licence or permit with you whenever you are driving.

Traffic keeps to the left. Drivers must yield (give way) to every vehicle approaching or crossing from their right. Seat belts are compulsory for all passengers. Helmets are compulsory for motorcyclists and sidecar passengers. Maximum speed limits are 50kmh (30mph) in built-up areas unless otherwise indicated, 100kmh (60mph) on open roads. Besides ice and snow, road hazards include slips, rock falls, possums, quail, flocks of sheep and herds of cows, so go carefully. If you should encounter animals

Ferries link the North and South Islands

on the road, take your time and edge through them, or get someone to walk ahead to clear a path for the vehicle.

Tolerance of drink driving is low in New Zealand – something that is well worth bearing in mind when visiting the wine regions and doing vineyard tasting tours. It is illegal to have a blood alcohol content of more than 0.05 percent for those over 20 years old, and 0.03 percent for those under 20. Driving under the influence of drugs is also illegal, and police make random stops, occasionally closing down entire roads to test drivers. It is also illegal to talk into a handheld mobile phone while driving.

Fuel costs: fuel is generally cheaper in cities than it is in country areas.

Roadside assistance: the New Zealand Automobile Association offers free services and privileges to members of accredited overseas motoring organisations. It also handles vehicle insurance. Through the Association you can make reservations for accommodation and the inter-island ferry. See its website, www.aa.co.nz, or contact one of the following offices: Auckland: 99 Albert Street, tel: 09-966 8919; Wellington: 342–52 Lambton Quay, tel: 04-931 9999; Christchurch: 114 Marshland Road, Shirley,, tel: 03-386 1090.

Car hire: to rent a car you will need an approved national or international driving licence. The minimum age is 21, and drivers under 25 sometimes have to pay more for insurance. Major international firms such as Avis, Hertz and Budget have offices in New Zealand, but local firms such as Apex can often offer cheaper deals. Hire cars range from NZ\$478–200 per day, with rates fluctuating seasonally and varying according to the length of rental. Camper vans cost from NZ\$230or less in low season to NZ\$620 for a six-berth in high season.

Note, however, that even if you take out a collision-damage waiver, you can still end up paying for the first NZ\$500 or NZ\$1,000 of any damage to your hire vehicle – whether you are responsible for the accident or not. However, several firms offer extra insurance to reduce your exposure to this insidious charge.

Chauffeur-driven vehicles are available for short or long trips. Taxi companies also provide the services of experienced driver-guides. Rates usually include basic mileage plus the driver's living expenses and vary according to the number of passengers.

Vaccinations

No vaccination certificates are needed for entry into New Zealand. However, if within three weeks of your arrival you develop any sickness such as a skin rash, fever and chills, diarrhoea or vomiting, you should consult a doctor.

Temuera Morrison in 'Once Were Warriors'

BOOKS AND FILM

New Zealand is a movie location scout's dream destination, needing little make-up or CGI to appear beguiling or otherworldly, with its active volcanoes, immense mountain ranges, gigantic glaciers, bubbling mud pools, wonderful waterfalls, voluptuous valleys and sprawling, surf-licked beaches. And this dramatic terrain has also proven to be fertile ground for writers, inspired by their unique surrounds to create world-class works of literature with a distinct Kiwi accent.

FILM

The savage beauty of New Zealand rushed into the global public's awareness in wide-screen shock-and-awe format in 2001, with the release of Peter Jackson's film, *The Fellowship of the Ring*. It was, of course, just the first instalment of a trilogy of epic cinematic renditions of English author J.R.R Tolkien's magnum opus, *The Lord of the Rings*, with *The Two Towers* (2002) and *The Return of the King* (2003) following hot on its heels. Between 2012 and 2014, Tolkien's earlier scene-setting book, *The Hobbit*, was made into a three-film prequel, with all the action once again shot on location in New Zealand.

Tolkien himself never visited New Zealand, but it's hard to imagine that there's anywhere more akin to the Middle-earth he dreamt up as a setting for his fantastic tales than this country, teetering on the southern periphery of the planet. Jackson exploited the backyard he grew up in to full and fabulous effect. The three *Lord of the Rings* films were shot concurrently over a period of 438 days in places including Tongariro National Park, and many sites around Queenstown and Wellington. With all the extras required, the project became one of the country's biggest employers during the production stages.

It's hard to think of another example of a film's shooting location becoming so synonymous with a travel destination, but New Zealand has starred on the big screen in other notable works. Prominent examples include Jackson's first critically acclaimed film – the Christchurch-set, true-crime story *Heavenly Creatures* (1994), which featured a young Kate Winslet – and Jane Campion's Palme d'Or-winning *The Piano* (1993), starring American actors Holly Hunter and Harvey Keitel alongside New Zealanders Sam Neill and Anna Paquin (whose performance won her an Academy Award for Best Supporting Actress at the age of 11).

The underbelly of New Zealand's Maori communities and some of the serious social problems that exist within them are the focus of the highly regarded 1994 film *Once Were Warriors*. Based

A hobbit house on set

on the writings of New Zealand author Alan Duff, it's a no-punches-pulled story about abuse, alcoholism, poverty, violence and gangs. Considerably more uplifting is the excellent 2002 film *Whale Rider*, set and filmed in Whangara on the east coast of the North Island. It stars 12-year-old Keisha Castle-Hughes, whose performance saw her become the youngest person ever nominated for an Academy Award for Best Actress.

The 2005 biographical film, *The World's fastest Indian*, features Anthony Hopkins playing New Zealand bike racer Burt Munro – who set several land speed records on his Indian Scout motorcycle in the 1950s and 60s – and was mostly shot around Invercargill and Southland, the most southerly part of the South Island.

In 2013, the brooding and brilliant crime drama *The Top of the Lake* – written and directed by Campion, and set and shot in Queenstown and Glenorchy – became the first miniseries ever screened at the Sundance Film Festival.

BOOKS

Beside the authors and works referenced above, which have been translated into films, New Zealand has produced several critically acclaimed writers.

One of Wellington's most famous daughters is Katherine Mansfield, author of several collections of highly regarded short stories, including *The Garden Party*. You can visit the two-storey family home where she was born in 1888, the Katherine Mansfield Birthplace (25 Tinakori Road; www.katherinemansfield.com; Tue–Sun 10am–4pm; charge) in the Wellington district of Thorndon.

Janet Frame's autobiography *An Angel at My Table* tells a story more extraordinary than fiction. Now regarded as one of New Zealand's most noted authors, Frame (real name Nene Janet Paterson Clutha) suffered years of psychiatric problems and was scheduled to have a lobotomy until her first published collection of short stories unexpectedly won a literary award and the procedure was abruptly cancelled. She went on to win a multitude of other awards during a prolific writing career, including the 1988 Commonwealth Writers Prize for her last novel, *The Carpathians*.

Later writers include Keri Hulme, a South Island author with mixed Maori and British heritage, whose first and only novel – an intricate, nuanced and at times dark story of love called *The Bone People* – won the Booker Prize in 1984. More recently, young Canadian/Kiwi author Eleanor Catton won the 2013 Man Booker Prize with her second book, the 832-page epic *The Luminaries*. The plot of the ingeniously structured novel revolves around the south coast goldfields of New Zealand's South Island and is set in 1866. Catton became the youngest person to ever win the illustrious Man Booker Prize at the age of 28.

ABOUT THIS BOOK

This *Explore Guide* has been produced by the editors of Insight Guides, whose books have set the standard for visual travel guides since 1970. With top-quality photography and authoritative recommendations, these guidebooks bring you the very best routes and itineraries in the world's most exciting destinations.

BEST ROUTES

The routes in the book provide something to suit all budgets, tastes and trip lengths. As well as covering the destination's many classic attractions, the itineraries track lesser-known sights, and there are also excursions for those who want to extend their visit outside the city. The routes embrace a range of interests, so whether you are an art fan, a gourmet, a history buff or have kids to entertain, you will find an option to suit.

We recommend reading the whole of a route before setting out. This should help you to familiarise yourself with it and enable you to plan where to stop for refreshments – options are shown in the 'Food and Drink' box at the end of each tour.

For our pick of the tours by theme, consult Recommended Routes for… (see pages 6–7).

INTRODUCTION

The routes are set in context by this introductory section, giving an overview of the destination to set the scene, plus background information on food and drink, shopping and more, while a succinct history timeline highlights the key events over the centuries.

DIRECTORY

Also supporting the routes is a Directory chapter, with a clearly organised A–Z of practical information, our pick of where to stay while you are there and select restaurant listings; these eateries complement the more low-key cafés and restaurants that feature within the routes and are intended to offer a wider choice for evening dining. Also included here are some nightlife listings and our recommendations for books and films about the destination.

ABOUT THE AUTHORS

This edition was updated by Malgorzata Anczewska, building on the work of Pat Kinsella. Pat is a British/Australian writer who has spent many months travelling the length and breadth of New Zealand – climbing its peaks, cycling and tramping its trails and generally exploring its many and varied corners, from the hidden backwaters to the most vibrant urban areas – all the time wondering why he doesn't live here full time.

This book builds on original content by Craig Dowling and Donna Blaber.

CONTACT THE EDITORS

We hope you find this Explore Guide useful, interesting and a pleasure to read. If you have any questions or feedback on the text, pictures or maps, please do let us know. If you have noticed any errors or outdated facts, or have suggestions for places to include on the routes, we would be delighted to hear from you. Please drop us an email at hello@insightguides.com. Thanks!

CREDITS

Explore New Zealand
Editor: Rachel Lawrence
Author: Patrick Kinsella
Head of Production: Rebeka Davies
Update Production: Apa Digital
Picture Editor: Tom Smyth
Cartography: original cartography
Berndtson & Berndtson, updated by Carte
Photo credits: 123RF 23, 84, 94/95, 137;
Alamy 90B, 136; Andy Belcher/Apa Pub-
lications 28, 31, 32/33, 37L, 40, 40/41,
44, 60, 64/65, 80, 88, 90/91, 92, 93, 93L,
94, 95L, 96, 100; Bay of Plenty Tourism
49L, 124; Canterbury Tourism 128; Chris
Cameron/Tourism NZ 29; christchurchnz.
com 119L; Design Hotels 105; Design
Hotels 104; Destination Rotorua 51, 55;
Getty Images 24, 25; Hanmer Springs 81;
Huka Lodge 19L; iStock 1, 6MC, 6BC, 7MR,
16/17, 22, 26/27T, 30, 32, 33L, 34, 36,
36/37, 44/45, 45L, 46/47, 47L, 48, 50,
56, 57, 60/61, 69L, 78/79, 82, 84/85,
85L, 97; Kiwi Encounter 83; Leonardo
102MC, 102MR, 108, 108/109, 109L,
110, 111, 112/113, 117; Millbrook Resort
102ML, 120/121; New Zealand Tourist
Board 35; NZ Tourism 7T, 7MR, 10, 16, 18,
18/19, 38, 39L, 38/39, 41L, 42, 43, 46,
48/49, 52, 52/53, 53L, 54, 58, 59, 61L,
62, 63, 64, 66, 70, 71, 72, 86/87, 89, 90,
98, 98/99, 99L, 100/101, 114, 114/115,
115L, 117L, 125, 126, 127, 129, 130,
131, 132, 133; Peter James Quinn/Apa
Publications 4ML, 4MC, 4MR, 4MR, 4MC,
4ML, 4/5T, 6TL, 6ML, 7M, 8ML, 8MC, 8ML,
8MC, 8MR, 8MR, 8/9T, 10/11, 11L, 12,
13L, 12/13, 14, 15, 17L, 20, 21L, 20/21,
26ML, 26MC, 26MR, 26ML, 26MC, 26MR,
65L, 67, 68, 68/69, 102ML, 102MR,
102MC, 102/103T, 134, 135; Skycity 106;
Sudima Hotels 116; Tourism Dunedin 73,
74, 75L, 74/75, 76, 77; Waitakere Estate
107; Wellington Tourism 118, 118/119,
122/123
Cover credits: Shutterstock
(main&bottom)

Printed by CTPS — China

All Rights Reserved
© 2018 Apa Digital (CH) AG and
Apa Publications (UK) Ltd
Second Edition 2018

DISTRIBUTION

UK, Ireland and Europe
Apa Publications (UK) Ltd
sales@insightguides.com
United States and Canada
Ingram Publisher Services
ips@ingramcontent.com
Australia and New Zealand
Woodslane
info@woodslane.com.au
Southeast Asia
Apa Publications (Singapore) Pte
singaporeoffice@insightguides.com
Worldwide
Apa Publications (UK) Ltd
sales@insightguides.com

SPECIAL SALES, CONTENT LICENSING AND COPUBLISHING

Insight Guides can be purchased in bulk
quantities at discounted prices. We can
create special editions, personalised jackets
and corporate imprints tailored to your needs.
sales@insightguides.com
www.insightguides.biz

INDEX

MAP LEGEND

● Start of tour

→ Tour & route direction

❶ Recommended sight

❷ Recommended restaurant/café

★ Place of interest

ℹ Tourist information

𝟏 Statue/monument

✉ Main post office

🚌 Main bus station

🕿 Viewpoint

　 Park

　 Important building

　 Hotel

　 Transport hub

　 Market/store

　 Pedestrian area

　 Urban area

INSIGHT ⦿ GUIDES
OFF THE SHELF

Since 1970, INSIGHT GUIDES has provided a unique perspective on the world's best travel destinations by using specially commissioned photography and illuminating text written by local authors.

Whether you're planning a city break, a walking tour or the journey of a lifetime, our superb range of guidebooks and phrasebooks will inspire you to discover more about your chosen destination.

INSIGHT GUIDES

offer a unique combination of stunning photos, absorbing narrative and detailed maps, providing all the inspiration and information you need.

PHRASEBOOKS & DICTIONARIES

help users to feel at home, when away. Pocket-sized with a free app to download, they go where you do.

CITY GUIDES

pack hundreds of great photos into a smaller format with detailed practical information, so you can navigate the world's top cities with confidence.

EXPLORE GUIDES

feature easy-to-follow walks and itineraries in the world's most exciting destinations, with our choice of the best places to eat and drink along the way.

POCKET GUIDES

combine concise information on where to go and what to do in a handy compact format, ideal on the ground. Includes a full-colour, fold-out map.

EXPERIENCE GUIDES

feature offbeat perspectives and secret gems for experienced travellers, with a collection of over 100 ideas for a memorable stay in a city.

www.insightguides.com